Lessons From Switzerland

Lessons From Switzerland

How might Britain go about business outside the EU?

Jonathan Lindsell

CIVITAS

First Published October 2015

© Civitas 2015
55 Tufton Street
London SW1P 3QL

email: books@civitas.org.uk

ISBN 978-1-906837-72-3

Independence: Civitas: Institute for the Study of Civil Society is a registered educational charity (No. 1085494) and a company limited by guarantee (No. 04023541). Civitas is financed from a variety of private sources to avoid over-reliance on any single or small group of donors.

All publications are independently refereed. All the Institute's publications seek to further its objective of promoting the advancement of learning. The views expressed are those of the authors, not of the Institute, as is responsibility for data and content.

Designed and typeset by
lukejefford.com

Printed in Great Britain by
Berforts Group Ltd
Stevenage, SGI 2BH

Contents

Author

Jonathan Lindsell joined Civitas in 2013 as EU research fellow after reading history at Trinity College, Oxford. His other Civitas publications include *Softening the Blow: Who gains from the EU and how they can survive Brexit* and 'The Norwegian Way: A case study for Britain's future relationship with the EU'. He has written for Vagenda, *The Independent*, Index on Censorship, Left Foot Forward and Open Democracy.

Acknowledgements

Many thanks to the colleagues, referees and respondents whose comments pointed the research in new directions and contributed to areas that would otherwise be deficient. Any remaining errors are, of course, my own.

List of Acronyms

CHF   Swiss franc
EC   European Commission, the EU's
           executive institution
EEA   European Economic Area, currently
           Iceland, Norway, Liechtenstein plus
           the EU
EEC   European Economic Community,
           the predecessor to the EU
EFTA   European Free Trade Association,
           currently Iceland, Norway,
           Liechtenstein, Switzerland
EU   European Union
Eurozone   Austria, Belgium, Cyprus, Estonia,
           Finland, France, Germany, Greece,
           Ireland, Italy, Latvia, Lithuania,
           Luxembourg, Malta, the Netherlands,
           Portugal, Slovakia, Slovenia, Spain
FDI   Foreign direct investment
FTA   Free trade agreement
GATS   General Agreement on Trade in Services
           (a WTO treaty)
GDP   Gross domestic product

IMF	International Monetary Fund
JETRO	Japanese External Trade Organisation
JSFTEPA	Japanese-Swiss Free Trade and Economic Partnership Agreement
LG/NLG	Liberalised goods/non liberalised goods
MAFF	Japanese Ministry of Agriculture, Forestry and Fisheries
MFN	Most favoured nation, a WTO tariff designation
OED	Observatory for Economic Complexity
OECD	Organisation for Economic Cooperation and Development
SCC	Swiss Chamber of Commerce and Industry
SECO	Swiss Secretariat for Economic Affairs
SME	Small and medium enterprises
TPP	Trans-Pacific Partnership
TRIPS	Agreement on Trade-Related Aspects of Intellectual Property Rights
TTIP	Transatlantic Trade and Investment Partnership
WTO	World Trade Organisation

Executive Summary

- If Britain left the European Union it would be free to organise its own trade deals. There is some debate as to whether this would be to Britain's advantage or whether it would then struggle on its own to secure the best terms. Lessons can be learned from Switzerland – which is not a member of the EU and has negotiated trade deals on its own – about how the UK might fare in such a scenario.

- Switzerland has a much smaller market to offer than Britain but has been able to secure advantageous terms in trade deals with economies much larger than its own. This is borne out well by close examination of its 2009 trade deal with Japan, from which Swiss exports have benefited significantly. Swiss exports of chocolate, cereal, cheese and watches to Japan all face lower tariffs now.

- UK trade would have much to gain if Britain took a similar approach to Switzerland, whose achievement has been considerable given Japan's historically protectionist approach, especially over food. Moreover, the EU has failed to conclude any sort of free trade agreement with Japan.

- Many possible trade partners are intimidated by the EU's great size, which could be a threat to their domestic industries. This can delay or halt EU negotiations, which are anyway slowed by competing internal demands. Britain alone would not be such a threat or suffer such internal division, but would still be an attractive market.

- Securing advantageous trade deals outside the EU cannot be taken for granted, however. The Swiss case illustrates the importance of having clear goals, a willingness to open protected sectors to competition and active participation in global trade bodies.

- If Britain left the EU, it should consider hiring experienced negotiators from non-EU countries that have already won major trade deals, such as Switzerland, Australia or South Korea. The Swiss deal with Japan took roughly six years to conclude from initial joint studies to coming into force.

- An independent Britain should also build on the Swiss strategy of keeping pace with or pre-empting the world's largest economies by closing deals with their prospective partners and contributing to global standards bodies. This is important to keep influence on major developments to world trading rules.

- The benefits of negotiating trade deals independently extend beyond trade. Diplomatic relations can also be enhanced through the independent negotiation of trade agreements. Good relations between Switzerland and Japan were carried on after their trade deal was signed and produced further agreements. Britain could use trade policy as a positive foreign policy tool.

Introduction

Those in favour of the UK's continued membership of the European Union marshal several arguments critical of exit. One of the most prominent is that Britain would not, as a lone state, have the economic or political power to negotiate the comprehensive free trade deals that the EU can with the world's leading economies.

This paper looks for lessons on how the UK might fare alone by using Switzerland as a case study. Switzerland is outside the EU and so conducts its own trade policy; it has free trade deals with China, Japan, Singapore, Canada and Hong Kong.[1] This would suggest that an independent Britain would be able to forge partnerships with important markets, indeed markets with which the EU has no agreement in place (China, Japan, Hong Kong). With countries like these, British trade goals like making foreign markets more open to UK services could be prioritised, whereas currently British aims must compete with those of other EU members.

However, critics argue that the Swiss examples are misleading because these trade deals are actually imbalanced in favour of the larger market. Would Brexit therefore mean Britain could be bullied into granting vast concessions to global competitors in exchange for little gain? This idea was briefly examined in the case of the Sino-Swiss trade deal (2014) in a previous Civitas publication.[2] The agreement is slightly in protectionist

China's favour, as might be expected from the most populous state and second largest economy in the world. However, the Swiss trading model shows how Britain might in fact be able to win significant tariff concessions, regulatory agreements, open investment prospects, and services market access that it would not enjoy as a member of the EU. An asymmetric trade deal can be beneficial to both partners. If it was not in Swiss interests, the Swiss parliament would not have ratified it. This does not mean the agreement struck was the best possible deal for Switzerland, but it was better than what Switzerland would have as an EU member.

The Sino-Swiss agreement, however, only came into force on 1 July 2014. It is of limited use in discovering British lessons on free trade effectiveness. The Swiss agreement with Japan, properly the Japanese-Swiss Free Trade and Economic Partnership Agreement (FTEPA), came into force on 1 September 2009, so presents much more data for evaluation.[3] It presents a useful case study for how the UK might be able to secure favourable trade deals should it leave the EU. The analysis presented below assumes for the sake of argument that if Britain voted to leave the EU then it would become responsible for negotiating its own free trade agreements while retaining free trade with the EU Single Market, similar to the circumstances of Switzerland or Norway.

Switzerland's relationship with Japan in particular helps shed light on whether an independent Britain could win deals with the world's major economies. When the deal began in 2009, Japan was (and remains) an extremely important market, the third largest in the world behind only America and China.[4] It is roughly $1 trillion wealthier than Germany.[5] It is also a developed nation with its own high regulatory standards and famously protected industries, meaning it provides an ideal opportunity to consider whether Britain could make quality agreements with hard-bargaining partners.[6]

This paper will consider several questions on the Swiss-Japanese Trade and Economic Partnership. First, is the deal actually good for the Swiss economy? Does it cover the goods and services that Switzerland has an interest in selling? Second, could a hypothetical Britain outside the European Union seek to replicate the deal? How should it go about negotiations, and how long would they take? What concessions might be considered?

This is not an argument for copying the Swiss-EU relationship. It simply uses Switzerland, as the best example of a non-EU state that has free trade in Europe and control of its own trade policy, to examine Britain's trade prospects if it leaves the EU.

Part 1

Switzerland, A Case Study

1

Background

Switzerland is not, and has never been, a member of the European Economic Community (EEC) or the European Union. In 1960 it was a founding member of the European Free Trade Association (EFTA), a counter-bloc led by the United Kingdom, which then included Austria, Denmark, Norway, Portugal and Sweden. Finland, Iceland and Liechtenstein later joined. This arrangement enabled free trade in industrial products between members but did not cover agricultural products or create a customs union with common external tariffs as the EEC did.

When the UK and Denmark joined the EEC in 1973, the remaining EFTA bloc signed a limited free trade agreement with the whole EEC group, meaning Switzerland kept free trade with the departing members and gained tariff-free access to West Germany, France, Holland, Italy, Belgium and Luxembourg. Other EFTA members later moved to join the EU.

When the EEC developed the Single Market in the 1980s, with its emphasis on rules harmonisation and decreasing barriers to trade, the remaining EFTA members negotiated a new arrangement to get full access to it, called the European Economic Area (EEA).[1] Switzerland took part in the negotiations. EEA membership was seen as a transitory step to EU accession.[2] However, the Swiss people rejected EEA membership in a referendum on 6 December 1992 by 50.3 per cent to 49.7 per cent. The Swiss government then suspended its EU accession process.

In 1994, Switzerland and the EU started alternative negotiations for a more comprehensive economic partnership than the 1972 free trade agreement, but separate to the EEA. These resulted in 10 bilateral treaties passed in two sets. They make a large amount of EU law relevant to Switzerland, or to Swiss exporters, and include the four freedoms of the EU – free movement of goods, of workers, of services and of capital. However, they do not directly cover agriculture – a sector Switzerland heavily subsidises – or grant full financial services access. The first set of bilaterals was signed in 1998 and applied in 2002. The second set was mostly signed in 2004 and applied from 2006 and later. Switzerland also contributes to some EU funds. The treaties are shown in Box 1.

Box 1: Switzerland's Bilateral Agreements with the EU

Bilateral I, agreements on:

Technical barriers to trade (also called non-tariff barriers)

Free movement of persons

Civil aviation – air traffic

Overland traffic

Agriculture

Public procurement

Scientific research

Bilateral II, agreements on:

Security and asylum (Dublin Accords) and passport free zone (Schengen system membership)

Cooperation in fraud pursuits (taxation on savings, pensions)

Europol policing

Final stipulations in open questions about processed agricultural goods, the environment, statistics sharing, media, education, care of the elderly, and services.

More cooperation and specific bilaterals have since been agreed, such as on the Galileo satellite project, and Switzerland aims to sign more agreements on the energy and financial markets.

Switzerland can, either on its own or with the remaining EFTA countries, negotiate free trade agreements independently of the European Commission (EC). Free trade agreements are defined by the World Trade Organization as having to cover over 90 per cent of all the concerned parties' trade, meaning some vulnerable sectors can be excluded by mutual agreement. The protected areas are often those that cause the most contention and delays.

The Swiss State Secretariat for Economic Affairs (SECO) writes:

> Switzerland currently has a network of 28 free trade agreements with 38 partners outside the EU. Switzerland normally concludes its FTAs together with its partners Norway, Iceland and Liechtenstein, in the framework of the European Free Trade Association (EFTA). Nevertheless, Switzerland has the possibility to enter into FTAs outside the EFTA framework as well, as it has been the case of Japan and China.[3]
>
> The aim of Switzerland's free trade policy is the improvement of the framework conditions for economic relations with relevant economic partners. The objective is to provide Swiss companies with an unobstructed, stable and non-discriminatory market access in these countries compared to their main competitors. Foreign trade policy measures aiming at further opening export markets are of great importance and in accordance with the stabilization policy pursued by the Federal Council.[3]

In wider strategic terms, the Swiss economics secretariat is concerned that 'a looming discrimination of Swiss service providers and investors in third country markets can be avoided' through the Swiss global trading approach:

> The Federal Council's foreign economic policy strategy adopted in 2004 established four criteria for the selection of prospective free trade partners: 1) the current and potential economic importance of the partner country, 2) the extent of existing or potential discrimination that Switzerland would suffer vis-à-vis its main competitors in the market concerned, 3) the willingness of the partner country to enter into negotiations, and 4) political considerations, especially the coherence with Swiss foreign policy objectives.[4]

The Swiss economics secretariat economist appears confident that this approach has preserved Swiss suppliers' non-discriminatory access to important third-country markets. [5] Japan is of course a prime example – Switzerland's deal with Japan is in effect while neither Washington nor Brussels look anywhere near concluding deals.

By contrast, EU member states have no direct control of free trade policy but must follow the EC's lead. There is considerable concern about the opportunity costs of EU-negotiated treaties since they have to meet the interests of all 28 members, as well as the new free trade partner country, meaning an individual EU state's priorities are compromised. A prime example of this is France vetoing film and video's inclusion in the EU-US trade agreement under discussion, the Transatlantic Trade and Investment Partnership (TTIP).[6]

Table 1: Swiss and EFTA Free Trade Agreements compared to EU free trade agreements

Partner Country	Year of Swiss agreement entry into force	Services included?	Year of EU agreement entry into force	Services included?
Syria			1977	X
Andorra			1991	X
Turkey	1992	X	1996	X
Israel	1993	√	2000	X
Faroe Islands	1995	X	1997	X
Palestinian Authority	1999	√	1997	X
Morocco	1999	√	2000	X
Mexico	2001	√	2000	√
Croatia (EU member 2013)	2002	√	2002/2005	2002 X / 2005 √
Jordan	2002	√	2002	X
Macedonia	2002	√	2001/2004	2001 X / 2004 √
Singapore	2003	√	Not yet in force	(√)
San Marino			2002	X
Chile	2004	√	2003/2005	2003 X / 2005 √
South Korea	2006	√	2011	X
Tunisia	2006	√	1998	X
Lebanon	2007	√	2003	X
South Africa	2008	√	2000	X
Egypt	2007	√	2004	X
South African Customs Union: South Africa, Botswana, Lesotho, Namibia, Swaziland	2008	√		
Japan	2009	√		
Canada	2009	√	Not yet in force	(√)
Albania	2010	√	2006/2009	2006 X / 2009 √
Serbia	2010	X	2010	√
Algeria			2005	X
Columbia	2011	√	2013	X
Peru	2011	√	2013	X

Table 1 Continued right

Table 1: Swiss and EFTA Free Trade Agreements compared to EU free trade agreements

Partner Country	Year of Swiss agreement entry into force	Services included?	Year of EU agreement entry into force	Services included?
Central American Common Market: Costa Rica, El Salvador, Guatemala, Honduras,			2013	X
Ukraine	2012	√	(Delayed to 2016)	(√)
Hong Kong	2012	√		
Montenegro	2012	√	2008/2010	2008 X / 2010 √
Panama & Costa Rica	2014	X	2013	X
Cooperation Council for the Arab States of the Gulf (GCC): Bahrain, Kuwait, Oman, Qatar, Saudi Arabia, United Arab Emirates	2014, suspended	√		
China	2014	√		

Source: Swiss Secretariat for Economic Affairs website, 'List of Free Trade Agreements of Switzerland' page , and European Commission website, Trade Policy section, 'Agreements' page

Either because of the emphasis on developing the internal market, or on expanding EU free trade through the accession of states in central or eastern Europe, the EU has been generally slower than Switzerland to conclude free trade deals. Switzerland has also been more successful in concluding trade deals that include free trade in services, a matter of particular interest to the United Kingdom. This is shown in Table 1.

It is therefore clear that, if the market access of these free trade agreements is comparable, then Switzerland is not disadvantaged by negotiating trade deals from a solo or EFTA position. Indeed, Switzerland has several important deals that the EU does not have – with China, Hong Kong, Japan, the Gulf Cooperation Council (suspended), the whole South African Customs Union and Singapore. These compare favourably to the market size of deals the EU has that Switzerland does not – Algeria, San Marino, Syria and Andorra. Moreover, 25 of the Swiss agreements cover services whereas only nine of the EU's do, and eight of those as a later development or not yet in force.

The Swiss situation is developing

Switzerland voted by a narrow margin to try to renegotiate the free movement pillar of the Swiss-EU bilaterals in early February 2014.[7] It is currently unclear how this will be resolved since the EU has refused any change to the free migration agreement, and the Swiss leadership is constitutionally obliged to follow the referendum's conclusion despite their wanting to keep the rest of the bilaterals, which would be thrown into jeopardy were Switzerland to unilaterally impose new border or employment controls. The Swiss will probably be polled again on this basis.

This does not, however, show that the UK could not fare as well as the Swiss. It is not related to Switzerland's ability to win trade deals with non-European countries, and it merely mirrors the exact debate Britain is currently having from within the EU. If anything, it suggests that, in or out, European migration will remain a thorny point.

This study does not assume that Britain recreates the exact Swiss model after leaving the EU. The only important elements, for the purposes of a meaningful comparison, are i) that Switzerland is not an EU member, ii) has privileged access to the Single Market, and iii) can negotiate its own free trade agreements. This much is also true of Iceland and Norway, and to a lesser extent, Mexico, South Africa and South Korea, and it is likely that Britain would gain those three elements after leaving the EU. The Swiss-Japanese deal was chosen as a case study not to advance the case for the specific Swiss model of EU relations, but because Switzerland has an economy and outlook close to that of Britain.

Rules of origin

Keeping up with global trading rules and major competitors is a priority for Switzerland. The US is currently conducting two trade deals with many of the world's important economies through the Trans-Pacific Partnership (TPP) with east Asian and Australasian states, and the Transatlantic Trade and Investment Partnership (TTIP) with the EU. If both of these are concluded then the trade rules of all the states involved are likely to be standardised, which would have an impact on global standards. Because Switzerland is not a prospective TTIP or TPP member, its diplomats need to pursue other available means of influencing world trade rules, such as the WTO and UN.

An important example of regulatory hegemony outside US control is the system of rules of origin. Free trade agreements contain provisions called rules of origin for the purpose of defining, for all kinds of goods, what percentage of an object's weight, value or construction must have taken place in a country for that country to count as its place of origin. Products need to conform to these rules to be counted as originating in one of the states party to a free trade agreement to benefit from the deal's tariff removal.

Rules of origin exist to stop transhipment. This is when an exporter in State C benefits from the preferential tariff rates that States A and B have through a free trade agreement, by selling to State B by moving a product into State A then selling it to B, while State C only has free trade with State A.

Some goods that a country exports will not actually meet the rules of origin since they are made of materials from abroad (a third country), or largely assembled abroad. These exports will then be taxed at the pre-FTA tariff rate, which between Switzerland and Japan would be the most favoured nation rates enforced by the World Trade Organisation. Exporting businesses may need to change their supply chains or construction processes to conform to the rules and benefit from the tariff reduction.[8] Sometimes exporters may simply be unaware that they could get a preferential tariff on their sales, or decide that the cost of checking their product line and producing the paperwork to show that they conform to the rules of origin is greater than the potential saving of the tariff reduction. For many goods exports, haulage and shipping companies will handle this paperwork, but it can be daunting for small businesses selling complicated products, which means that the potential benefits of a trade deal are not always realised.

These rules are not standardised across the world. This means that different free trade agreements come with different rules of origin, requiring exporters to conform to multiple sets of rules at once or forgo the tariff benefits of a free trade agreement. There are different requirements for different classes of product: electronic equipment does not have the same requirements as confectionery, which does not have the same requirements as finished clothing. For example, assume Switzerland is selling Japan a widget. According to the Swiss-Japanese rules, assume 90 per cent of the raw materials that went into that widget must be Swiss. However, to sell the same widget to the EU, assume only 75 per cent of the materials must be Swiss but also the materials' final construction into the widget must have taken place in Switzerland. To conform to both, a Swiss widget manufacturer must use at least 90 per cent Swiss raw materials, and complete the main construction in Switzerland.

Given how many free trade agreements there already are in the world, and how divergent, rules of origin contribute to a trend in which world trade is not seen as getting simpler, but rather getting extremely complex since there are so many bespoke requirements between individual states or groups. This exacerbates the problem of different countries' markets having differing product regulations.

All else being equal, then, a business looking to build a new factory is likely to favour a country that not only has a lot of free trade agreements in force, but a lot of free trade agreements with similar rules of origin. A Swiss researcher, Matthias Schaub, found that although there are 11 states that can be considered what he calls 'FTA hubs' in that they have a lot of trade deals, of these 11 only the EU, India, Japan, Mexico and Switzerland have homogenous rules of origin across their agreements. Large economies including the US and China do not have this important benefit.

Of those identified, the most dominant rules of origin templates come from the EU and India. Schaub notes that economy size alone is not a key determinant in whether a state has similar rules of origin in free trade agreements, or America would surely be the most dominant. He sees Switzerland as an anomaly, because it is fairly small, and attributes its homogeneity to copying EU rules of origin in those cases wherein the

EU negotiated a free trade deal with a third party before Switzerland did.[9] Presumably Swiss rules of origin resemble European ones even in the opposite cases, where the Swiss negotiate the deal first, to preserve the European-Mediterranean standard template.[10]

The recent Swiss economy and currency

A brief note on the recent fortunes of the Swiss economy is useful as context in evaluating the impact of the Swiss-Japanese deal.

Being an advanced economy in the middle of Europe, Switzerland is closely linked to the fortunes of the rest of Europe and to the US. It experienced a growth slowdown in the aftermath of the 9/11 attacks along with the rest of the West, but revived growth with a series of reforms between 2003 and 2008.

The Swiss franc (CHF) is Switzerland's currency, controlled by the Swiss National Bank (SNB). The franc had until recently been considered a safe haven currency on account of its stability and low inflation. This is partly thanks to Switzerland's aversion to high public debt and tight rules on federal spending.

Switzerland and Swiss investments were affected by the 2007-8 financial crisis, but not so badly as other European states. The independence and strength of the franc made it attractive to many Europeans and international investors worried by the instability of Greece, Ireland and Portugal, who used Switzerland as a safe retreat, which caused the franc to climb to USD 1.10 (CHF0.91 per USD) in March 2011, then USD1.30 (CHF0.769 per dollar) by August 2011, and came close to parity with the euro.

This was seen as a huge overvaluation of the franc, and had severe effects on the economy since exports to the eurozone dropped off because they were too expensive and the tourism industry suffered. Some Swiss citizens would purposefully cross the borders to Italy, Germany or France for domestic shopping. Short-term Swiss government debt was pushed to negative yields for the first time in August 2011.[11]

After traditional attempts to curb the franc's strength, such as boosting liquidity and cutting interest rates, had failed, on 6 September 2011 the SNB announced its intention to peg (cap) the franc at a minimum rate of 1.20CHF/1EUR. At the time, the exchange rate was 1.095 CHF/EUR, so the move to devalue the franc required the SNB to confirm its preparation 'to buy foreign currency in unlimited quantities'. The force of this intervention had the desired effect and quickly sent the franc plunging to 1.22/EUR, while its value against the dollar lost nine per cent in just 15 minutes.[12]

The franc remained below the SNB's target (i.e. meeting or exceeding it) for the next three years. However in late 2014 the euro again appeared extremely fragile and began falling, linked to the fall in the oil price and hence the Russian rouble's collapse, and again fears over Greece as the anti-austerity party Syriza looked likely to win the Greek general election. In December 2014, the SNB introduced negative interest rates on commercial bank deposits to support the CHF ceiling.

However, the euro continued to decline and on 15 January 2015 the SNB abandoned its ceiling policy in an unforeseen announcement. This was because, pegged to the euro, the CHF had continued to fall against the dollar since 2011, meaning that overall it was not unsustainably overvalued by 2015. The move caused a serious market shock in the stock and currency markets as the franc swiftly rose against the euro and dollar. In a few minutes the euro went from buying 1.20 francs to buying just 0.8052, but it later recovered to buy 1.04. The negative commercial banking rate was also cut again from -0.25 per cent to -0.75 per cent.[13]

The Swiss franc has, then, gone through several twists and turns over the period when economists would expect to see the effects of the Swiss-Japanese deal. These changes naturally affect investor confidence as well as bilateral trade due to price fluctuations – and that is not to mention the Fukushima Daiichi disaster in 2011, which caused serious problems for the Japanese economy at the same time.

Switzerland as a model for Britain

There are groups and politicians that argue that Switzerland is a poor example for Britain's trade prospects outside the EU, and it is their arguments this paper addresses. For example, a summary paper by LSE academics supposes that eventual EU free trade deals with America and Japan will be superior to those the Swiss or British could negotiate alone.[14] The Centre for European Reform argues that the Swiss-Chinese free trade agreement proves that small countries do not have the clout to negotiate deals as equals, so will necessarily be sidelined or poorly treated:

> For many countries, negotiating a free trade deal with the UK would not be as important as an FTA with the EU, given the difference in market size. Furthermore, the UK's administrative resources could be overstretched if it had to pursue several negotiations simultaneously. [15]

The Centre for European Reform authors also make the point that the UK, being a fairly open economy, does not have the leverage that comes either from large markets or high tariffs, compared to Europe. However, size is a double-edged sword when negotiating FTAs, since economies as large as the US or the EU can daunt partners like Japan, which fear their own producers would be threatened, so concede less. The EU and China nearly escalated a dispute over solar panel exports to a trade war as recently as 2013.[16] This hardly shows that the EU is a compelling champion of free trade.

The group British Influence also disagrees with the Swiss free trade agreement argument:

> Germany, an EU and Euro member exported 5 times as much as we did to Brazil, and over 3 times as much as we did to China. The EU doesn't hold us back from emerging markets - our own policies do. What's more, being part of the EU gives us access to Free Trade deals with countries like South Africa, Mexico and South Korea - access we would lose if we left the EU.[17]

Such an argument actually dodges the main justification for free trade agreements – that they help exports grow faster and more profitably. No economist argues that free trade is the only means by which trade can grow, or that the UK economy is already perfectly structured to export. That does not mean it cannot improve – indeed, in the next paragraph, British Influence goes on to celebrate the benefits of EU free trade agreements with South Korea and South Africa. Readers will be able to decide for themselves whether Switzerland provides Britain with a good model for trading outside the EU.

2

Negotiating the Swiss-Japanese trade deal

A key question for considering Britain's place in the world economy is: how seriously would major economies take proposals for closer trading relationships?

Academics David Chiavacci and Patrick Ziltener from the University of Zurich conducted a study of Japanese attitudes to the announcement of Swiss-Japanese negotiations in the media in 2007, before the agreement was finalised or in force. They summarised their findings:

> A first group, taking a narrow economic perspective on FTAs, does not object to an FTA with Switzerland, but regards it, at best, as of secondary importance because of the limited economic effects to be expected. A second group, which is primarily concerned with the interests of the Japanese farming and fishery sectors, is supportive of an FTA with Switzerland because of its foreseeable little impact on Japan's primary sector of industry. In the long-term strategic, political-economic perspective of a third group, an FTA with Switzerland is regarded as of high potential as a door to the European market and an ideal case for an FTA with an advanced industrial economy.[1]

The third group is characterised as Japan's socioeconomic elite, so the group most important in defining the country's policy direction.

Box 2:
The Swiss-Japanese agreement timetable

Joint feasibility studies in 2003-4 and 2005-6

First negotiation round, May 2007

Thereafter seven more rounds up to signing, February 2009

Entered into force, September 1, 2009

The negotiation took four years if counted from the October 2005 agreement to set up a joint study group, or two if counted from the January 2007 agreement between Swiss President Micheline Calmy-Rey and Japanese Prime Minister Shinzo Abe to start formal negotiations. JETRO and SECO, the two countries' trade and economics organisations, had been conducting joint feasibility studies since 2002.[2]

Japan used to rely on multilateral agreements conducted through the WTO to bring down the world's tariffs. In the mid-2000s it accepted that bilateral deals could also be important to helping trade, but Japan's new trade agreements were almost all with east Asian states, partially in an attempt to keep up with China and South Korea.[3] This hints at the height of the Swiss achievement in getting a deal. This impression is reinforced by the authors' discussion of the Japanese Ministry for Agriculture, Forestry and Fisheries (MAFF), which has been a symbol for protectionist resistance to deep trade agreements. The ministry's opposition to liberalising food trade with Mexico nearly collapsed that deal – Mexico's nominal GDP was $1.295 trillion, more than twice the size of Switzerland's, yet still Mexico almost failed to conclude a deal and ended up with a compromise deal after a 16-month delay.[4]

Another illustration of the difficulties facing the Swiss negotiation effort was discord on the Japanese side:

> Japanese mass media severely criticize this situation regarding the complex composition of Japanese FTA delegations and [the] different and contradicting positions of involved ministries, which impede the formulation of a coherent Japanese FTA policy… former Prime Minister Koizumi played a pivotal role in the establishment of FTAs as new instruments in Japan's foreign trade policy.[5]

This observation implies several lessons for Britain: that the government should have a settled idea of negotiation red lines before talks begin, and that a minister should be the public face of negotiations, coordinating different departments. This will be explored further in Part Two.

Returning to Japanese perceptions of the negotiations, it is interesting to note that the Japanese public thought of Switzerland as a rural idyll, and was largely unaware of its strengths in innovation, engineering, finance and electronics. Essentially, it was not seen as economically significant. Chiavacci and Ziltener make no mention of a dearth of Swiss negotiating clout, or of the Japanese government presuming it can force unequal terms on the smaller country. The idea simply seems not to have come up. The widespread Japanese perception of Switzerland as a mountainous beauty spot, rather than a high quality production line, had several effects, reducing public interest in the negotiations as a whole, and limiting the level of industrial threat the Japanese public felt from the deal.

Since agriculture (and associated food, drink and seafood products) is so often a sticking point in free trade agreement negotiations, it is worth dwelling on the Japanese agriculture ministry's position before the Swiss-Japanese deal was agreed. Chiavacci and Ziltener quoted Japanese writer Yasushi Satô:

> The ratio of agricultural products of all imports from Switzerland is only 1.4%. MAFF's view is that even if customs duties for agricultural products should be reduced, it would only have a small impact on agriculture.[6]

This was why the Japanese agriculture ministry was relaxed about dealing with Switzerland and using the trade and economic partnership as an opportunity to show it was not implacable in its opposition to trade deals. Smaller states like Switzerland are apparently much better suited for such a demonstration than those on the scale of the EU – or the US, which is struggling to cut tariffs on agriculture and automobiles in the Trans-Pacific Partnership negotiations.[7] The academics also point out that Japan and Switzerland were already partners in a World Trade Organisation bloc, the G-10 group.[8]

Chiavacci and Ziltener also show why many of Japan's political economic elite supported the deal. They quote the English-language paper *Japan Times* in an interview with a Japanese official:

> 'We're looking to Switzerland because, well, it's in Europe,' a Foreign Ministry official who requested anonymity said when asked why the Alpine country was a potential partner. An agreement with Switzerland would offend no major lobby group, making it 'low-risk, low-return', he explained.[9]

This official clearly did not mean that Switzerland was a potential partner because it would give Japanese goods tariff-free access to the Single Market by simply selling them through Switzerland, because the rules of free trade deals preclude this, as discussed already. Switzerland's access to the Single Market would be useful from a Japanese perspective mainly for Japanese companies building subsidiaries in Switzerland, which could then take advantage of Switzerland's privileged position in Europe. Chiavacci and Ziltener comment themselves on this strategic choice:

> Because an FTA between the EU and Japan was regarded by many as very difficult and, therefore, to be very unlikely realized in the next years, an FTA with Switzerland as bridge between Japan and Europe was regarded of central importance and as a counterbalance to trade blocs building tendencies. [sic][10]

This highlights Britain's opportunity. The Japanese were aware that to use this Swiss bridge, they needed to set up subsidiaries in Switzerland to sell to Europe, something the deal would make simpler. They anticipated that a deal would, then, lead to increased foreign direct investment in Switzerland.[11] This cannot, however, have been Japan's only incentive to pursue the deal. Japan has signed trade agreements with other countries that are small like Switzerland but have no Single Market access, including Australia, Chile, and Peru.[12] All of these countries have smaller economies than Britain, no privileged EU access, yet seem to have done well in brokering trade agreements with leading economies.

3

The deal in detail

The Swiss-Japanese Free Trade and Economic Partnership Agreement is a second-generation trade agreement, which means it does not deal exclusively with tariff reduction. Instead, it removes obstacles to all kinds of trade, covering rules and regulations, intellectual property, consumer rights, competition, digital law and data handling. This is important because Britain has a lot to gain in improving services access around the world as well as goods.[1]

The authors of the Japanese perspectives study specifically looked at the question of migration to Japan, a country historically wary of immigration levels:

> [I]nterviewees hoped that a liberalization of the movement of highly-qualified specialists and business people between Switzerland and Japan would be included into an FTA as this could simplify and stimulate knowledge transfer and cooperation between the two countries [plus] knowledge transfer and cooperation.[2]

Japan agreed to this limited stipulation, whereas it became a sticking point in negotiations with east Asian countries which aimed at great access to the Japanese labour market for their workers.[3]

The Swiss deal covers migration rights between the trade partners. This is very different from EU/EEA free movement and does not open up either state's general employment market or include any provisions for citizenship. It covers only those who stay temporarily and essentially applies to businesspeople.[4]

This underlines the issues explored in the background section – that modern trade deals usually entail a number of elements such as regulations agreed outside parliament and limited migration, that may not be attractive to some UK voters, at least if they are achieved through harmonisation rather than mutual recognition of standards. The facilitation of business professional migration may not be contentious in itself, but could contribute to overall annual net immigration policies, which would inevitably affect the policies of parties with net immigration targets, especially if such clauses were agreed with multiple large countries like America, Brazil and China.

Iconic food products

In strict tariff terms, it is notable that tariffs on many products sold between the two countries were already low before the deal. Although under Most Favoured Nation (MFN) schedules both countries had some tariffs of over 600 per cent of product value on specific agricultural products, more than 95 per cent of total imports of some product groups were already duty free:[5] for Japan, cotton, petrol, machinery, transport equipment; for Switzerland, cotton and petrol. The most protected product types (less than 5 per cent of the group duty free under MFN) were animal products, fish, and clothing for Japan; animal products, dairy products, sugars and confectionery, textiles, clothing, leather and footwear for Switzerland. Overall, there were large areas where concessions could be made, but also high value product types that were already traded freely thanks to previous World Trade Organisation agreements.

The agreement certainly seems to cover many of the goods the Swiss would want to sell into previously protected areas of the Japanese market. The Swiss Chamber of Commerce and Industry (SCC) noted that 'almost all tariffs on industrial goods are dismantled', although for a small number, these tariffs are reduced gradually or after a transitional period. This gradual approach to making trade easier is normal for sensitive product types. Agricultural goods have their tariffs removed on a selected range, but this range includes emblematic products like Swiss cheese specialities, dried meat, chocolate and wine. Switzerland's concessions here include ornamental Bonsai plants, high quality fruit, sake (rice wine) and cigarettes.[6]

By looking at the annexes to the treaty, we can see some of the specific concessions Switzerland won:

- The tariff on natural cheeses falls from the rate other countries pay (the MFN rate) of 29.8 per cent, down to 14.9 per cent in steps over six years, while the total quota grows from 600 metric tons to 1,000. An attached schedule specifically includes Emmental, Gruyère, Raclette and other cheeses with registered Swiss origins.

- The tariff on sweets other than those containing cocoa or chewing gum falls from 25 per cent to 20 per cent for a 100 metric ton quantity.

- Tariffs on different chocolate and cocoa preparation products gradually fall to zero, such as defatted cocoa paste, which carries a 10 per cent tariff for the rest of the world.

- Cocoa powder without sweeteners also falls to zero from 12.9 per cent over an eight-year period, while powder with sweeteners falls from 29.8 per cent (MFN) to 15 per cent (first year of the Swiss-Japanese deal) to zero over 11 years.

- Chocolate slabs of over 2kg, usually taxed at 29.8 per cent, falls to between 17 per cent and 23.8 per cent according to composition.

- Finished chocolate, usually taxed at 10 per cent to 29.8 per cent (if it has a filling), falls to 8 per cent within a 1,500 ton quota.

- Breakfast cereal, usually taxed between 11.5 – 19.2 per cent or 26.6 - 49¥/kg, falls to 8.1 per cent.

- Waffles and wafers, usually taxed at 18 per cent, fall to 12.6 per cent.

- Japan already did not tax many relevant products such as pearls, diamonds, precious and semi-precious stones, gold and base metals, watches and clocks. The zero tariffs are eliminated in the deal, meaning Japan could not tax these items arising from Switzerland even if it later chose to for the rest of the world.

- Some jewellery benefited – finished articles of jewellery of silver or other precious metals falls from 5.2 per cent to zero over 6-11 years. Watch chains fall from 5.4 per cent to zero over 11 years. Similarly leather watch-straps (an area of agricultural protection) fall from 16 per cent to zero over eight years.[7]

This gives a flavour of the concessions the Swiss-Japanese deal contained for Switzerland in some of

Japan's most protected product areas. A perfect deal from the Swiss perspective would see all such tariffs completely eliminated on the day the agreement came into force. It is clear that the Japanese government remained cautious about removing all protection from these areas, but still gave Swiss exports a trading advantage against Belgian chocolate and French cheese. Swiss interests were served in other areas – tariffs on inorganic chemicals, organic chemicals, pharmaceuticals and fertilisers were entirely eliminated. Many chemicals were already imported freely, but many others faced tariffs of 3-6 per cent and some specific tariff lines were as high as 17 per cent, or included very considerable charges based on weight. (For example, some alkaloids carry a charge of $5025.6 per kg, steroids over $500 per kg, and hormones over $3600 per kg.)[8]

Switzerland did not open everything to Japanese exporters heedlessly. A seminar by Michiaki Watanabe, director general of the Switzerland branch of the Japanese external trade organisation, addressed their fears over levels of radioactivity in Japanese food products and outlined which foods, from which areas, were being prohibited. At the same time, the presentation celebrated the deal for eliminating tariffs on miso paste, soy sauce, persimmon, melons, sake and ginger, decreasing tariffs on rice cakes and udon noodles, and eliminating quotas (but not tariffs) on a variety of fruits.[9]

A country's tariff schedule contains thousands of different product lines with different protections, all of which are available on the World Trade Organisation website for those more interested in the detail of complex machinery preferential tariffs.

Deciding whether Swiss concessions are greater than Japanese ones, whether the tariff section of the deal is unbalanced, is strongly subjective. The simple fact that the same tariffs are not removed at the same rate for each country proves nothing since of course it matters more to the Swiss than the Japanese to cut tariffs on chocolate, and more to the Japanese for the Swiss to cut tariffs on sake. Which country benefits more from the deal in the long run is future-dependent and cannot really be known by the negotiators. Looking at the tariff concessions of Japan on iconic Swiss exports, it certainly looks as though the deal was carried out as an agreement between peers, not the Japanese forcing Swiss markets open with scant concessions of their own.

Non-tariff benefits

The Swiss Chamber of Commerce and Industry also highlights the benefits of going beyond the World Trade Organisation's services rules in several areas, including financial services, telecommunications, domestic regulation of services, mutual recognition of service supplier qualifications and sector-specific provisions. There are provisions on digital signatures and online consumer protection, digital products and electronic certificates.

The agreement also covers provisions on copyright protection, trademarks, designs and patents, new plant certification (genetics), geographic indicators, confidentiality, fair competition and the enforcement of intellectual property rights.[10] This illustrates how deeply a second generation free trade agreement works, going beyond simple tariff lowering. It is interesting to note that the Swiss Chamber of Commerce and Industry makes no complaint of the deal being unbalanced – the organisation's tone is optimistic about the deal. Similarly Swiss Economics Minister Doris Leuthard claimed that the deal was the most important Switzerland has signed since the 1972 EU free trade agreement, and especially 'important for export companies, particularly chemical, pharmaceutical, watch and machine industries'.[11]

The text of the deal shows it is an evolving agreement. Article 88 ensures that investors in either state should not find themselves with less favourable conditions than third parties, if the third parties and Japan or Switzerland conclude more favourable deals. For example, when the Trans Pacific Partnership concludes, Japan may grant better investment conditions to America and the Pacific rim states – Article 88 would trigger the two governments to negotiate to amend the Swiss-Japanese deal up to that level (presumably in both directions).

Likewise Article 94 sets out rules for settling investor-state disputes through international law tribunals or arbitration. Such rules have become standard practice in free trade agreements and investment agreements, but have recently come under scrutiny and criticism for their inclusion in the Trans Pacific Partnership and TTIP, mainly for their complicated, secretive nature and the possibility of using the threat of a tribunal (and subsequent fine) to intimidate governments away from tightening or amending regulations in areas like labour law, environmental protection and public health.[12] However, Article 94 does not seem to have caused any problems for either partner thus far.

Diplomatic advantages

Because the Swiss-Japanese deal is an ongoing relationship with several review clauses, a little-noted benefit of the deal is ongoing positive diplomatic relations at the highest level. This could mean that the modest tariff decreases on some Swiss products could grow later on. Not only does continued dialogue demonstrate commitment to ironing out the problems that arise from implementing the free trade agreement, and even enhancing it, but the meetings also give the two governments further opportunities for cooperation.

A different presentation given by Michiaki Watanabe, from the Japanese external trade organisation, set out all the extra agreements between the two countries just a year after signing:

- Agreement on Cooperation in Science and Technology

- Protocol amending the Convention between Japan and Switzerland for the Avoidance of Double Taxation with respect to Taxes on Income

- Memorandum on establishing a framework for intensified cooperation and a bilateral policy dialogue

- Agreement on Social Security[13]

A more recent example of this close relationship was when Johann Schneider-Ammann, head of Switzerland's Federal Department of Economic Affairs, Education and Research, travelled to Japan to review the deal five years on and met four Japanese minsters and the deputy governor of the Bank of Japan in 2014.[14]

The Swiss brokered meaningful concessions in their deal with Japan. They gained a competitive tariff advantage over other European exporters in iconic products such as cheese, chocolate and waffles. The deal includes important clauses on selling services in Japan, on investor protection, intellectual property and digital rights. Finally, the initial 2009 agreement has fostered a period of closer diplomatic cooperation between the two countries.

4

The economic impact of the deal

Using the deal and rules of origin

The first important question to bear in mind when evaluating the impact of an FTA is: how many traders are actually using it?

Importers and exporters of goods do not automatically benefit from free trade agreements. They have to prove that the good they are selling originates from their own country (a Swiss watchmaker needs to prove that she is indeed selling Swiss watches, not Austrian ones). This is fully explained in the introduction. As noted, some exporters may be unaware that they could gain preferential tariffs on their sales, or have products that do not conform to the origin rules, or calculate that the cost of checking their product lines and producing the paperwork to show that they conform to the rules is greater than the potential saving of the tariff reduction. It can be daunting to make such adjustments for small businesses selling complicated products.

Measuring the impact of the trade and economic partnership must first look at how much it is actually used, before looking at the impact on state-state trade patterns. Using information from the Swiss Federal

Customs Office, a study by the University of Zurich looked at Japanese use of the trade and economic partnership in the 16 months after the agreement came into force (looking at Swiss use would require Japanese customs data). They found that use of the trade and economic partnership was between 24.1 per cent and 31.9 per cent across Japan's eight biggest export industries (which account for 99 per cent of exports to Switzerland). However, uptake varied dramatically by industry, so the automotive sector had about 73 per cent uptake, textiles 39.5-47.0 per cent, but watches and precious metals both below 2 per cent.[1]

Taken month by month, uptake appears to be increasing. Use of the trade partnership was only about 20 per cent in the first five months after the deal came into force, but 30-45 per cent between February and December 2010. The Zurich study's authors also compare the use rate of older Swiss free trade agreements and suggest that 'the current utilization level of around 40 per cent leaves room for future increases potentially even outgrowing the figures currently attained by South Korean exports'.[2] We cannot assume that Swiss use of the preferential tariffs was an identical mirror to that of Japanese exports, but it is fair to suggest that since the economies are of a similar sophistication and they are dealing with the same agreement, Swiss exporters would have adapted to the new rules of origin at a comparable rate.

Switzerland Global Enterprise, a Swiss government body for boosting trade, found 54.5 per cent of surveyed companies that were already exporting to Japan were supported by the FTA, and a further 15.2 per cent wanted to take advantage of it in the future.[3] A later Switzerland Global Enterprise report from 2014 found this had improved to 62.7 per cent.[4] As explored already, many tariffs were reduced gradually over several years – 16 years on some products – so it is understandable that use would still be low and growing just two years after the deal came into force. This is likely to be indicated in the analysis of trade flows in the next section.

A Swiss doctoral student, Matthias Schaub, argues in another study that the 'fact that mainly large companies are found to utilize FTAs should be of a concern to policy makers, especially if trade policy in the form of FTAs is supposed to address the topic of internationalization of SMEs (small and medium sized enterprises).' There are, he argues, relatively high initial fixed costs to benefitting from free trade agreements, some of which governments could do more to provide information about or help with. This argument is backed up by the Switzerland Global Enterprise article, which notes that 30.4 per cent of companies surveyed were not using the Swiss-Japanese deal in 2011 because it is too difficult/burdensome (*beschwerlich*), especially regarding the rules of origin, or because they do not know of the advantages.[5] Schaub asserts that for the Swiss-Japanese deal, 'the promotion of the authorized exporter scheme as a fundamental precondition to automate the FTA-process is of utmost importance', as the main way small businesses will use the deal rather than simply paying MFN tariffs.[6]

He favours multilateral free trade agreements over bilateral ones since rules of origin for the former usually allow what is called 'cumulation of origin', which lets a country treat product materials from other signatories as its own. This means that for a product to qualify for a deal's preferential tariff, it can have been assembled in the territory of any of that deal's signatories, and can include raw materials from any of them. Switzerland is part of the Pan-Euro-Mediterranean Protocol on Rules of Origin which covers the EU and EFTA countries as well as many in North Africa and the Middle East. This allows a Swiss manufacturer to class materials from Algeria, Israel or France as if they were Swiss. This helps to build up the percentage of the product that is classed as Swiss, so it is more likely to qualify for reduced tariffs under rules of origin.[7]

Schaub also makes several important points of caution managing optimism. He explains that there are several reasons that an FTA might not have a significant effect on trade flows beyond simple lack of use. '[I]f price-elasticity of demand is too small to create a consumption effect… there is no increase in trade' (although consumers will be slightly better off). This means that if a good has a small tariff removed, the difference to prices on the shop-floor might not be enough to affect the volume of sales.[8]

The second reason an effective free trade agreement might not influence trade flows is simple – 'companies may choose not to pass on the tariff savings to the consumers but to keep it in the form of a higher profit margin'. Of course, this extra profit might be retrenched later in the form of marketing or product improvement, which could have a long-term trade effect, but might simply be kept by the company.[9] This is indicated in a *Japan Times* article, which observes that Emmental and Gruyére prices do not seem to have come down in Japan despite nine months having elapsed since the agreement came into force.[10] Similarly, Switzerland Global Enterprise noted in 2011 that the free trade agreement had paid off for most businesses in revenue and/or profit.[11] Businesses profiting from the agreement would not necessarily be seen as a bad thing by the states involved in the free trade agreement, but this is still notable as a reminder that even free trade agreements that are highly used might not show much difference in trade flows or consumer savings.

Trade effects

The Swiss Secretariat for Economic Affairs, the Swiss version of UK Trade and Industry, presents the Swiss-Japanese deal as an important triumph on their website. Talking about all Swiss free trade agreement partners other than the EU, the Swiss economics secretariat claims 'Swiss exports to FTA partners grow almost twice as fast as those to the rest of the world' and boasts 'cheaper imports for both consumers and producers; improved procurement as well as supply security... an average annual growth rate of Swiss foreign direct investment in partner countries of 18 percent'.[12] This was echoed in an article by Roland Meier of Switzerland Global Enterprise, reviewing the deal after five years: 'Bottom line, Swiss importers of goods from Japan have saved CHF 41 million in customs duties thanks to the FTA... They are currently saving about CHF 10 million each year.' Meier noted Swiss citizens were especially benefitting from cheaper Japanese cars.[13]

Another indicator of an agreement's success according to the Swiss economics secretariat is export diversification. As 'the share of Switzerland's top five export industries has fallen in almost every country' after trade deals with those countries came into effect, the Swiss economics secretariat is confident that falling tariff barriers allow other industries to compete better in foreign markets. At the time of publication, the Swiss-Japanese deal had not been in force long enough for the Swiss economics secretariat to show this diversification with Japan itself, but their table demonstrates this effect in older agreements. For example, the category 'watches and clocks' breaks into the top five exports to Chile, Mexico and Morocco after their respective agreements came into force.[14]

Discussion of free trade agreement benefits is often limited to macroeconomic modelling and intangible changes in trade and investment flows. The Swiss economics secretariat, however, points out that its FTA programme has also directly affected Swiss individuals and companies:

> [C]onsumers gained from increased imports, lower prices and increased product variety. Manufacturers gained from advantageous prices for intermediate goods and improved access to raw materials which are not available in Switzerland. In addition, domestic companies are able to import capital goods (e.g. machinery or electronic equipment) at more advantageous prices.[15]

Swiss businesses responded positively, noting not only profits and turnover increases, but a particular appreciation for the mutual recognition of standards and certificates, and the improved protection of intellectual property.[16] The Japanese equivalent of the Swiss economics secretariat, Japan External Trade Organization, presents a slightly more confusing picture of the deal's impact. Figure 1 below uses JETRO data to show the changes in product group imports before and after the deal, to see if it confirms the Swiss economics secretariat's claims.

As discussed in the previous section, Switzerland achieved notable tariff reduction in food exports, so the

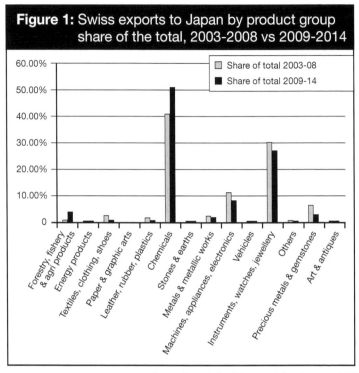

Figure 1: Swiss exports to Japan by product group share of the total, 2003-2008 vs 2009-2014

Source: Swiss Federal Customs Administration, 2015

considerable increase in sales of forestry, fishery and agricultural products confirms success. Tariffs on inorganic chemicals, organic chemicals and pharmaceuticals were entirely eliminated by the deal, so their growing share conforms to expectations that tariff reduction should boost trade. Many chemicals were already imported freely, but many others faced tariffs of 3-6 per cent and some specific tariff lines were as high as 17 per cent, or very considerable charges based on weight (above).[17]

Trade 2009-2014 was greater overall than 2003-2008, so a drop in the share of product types like electronics and jewellery does not imply a serious drop in actual sales. Electronics sales were slightly down and watch/jewellery sales, slightly up – and in 2015 Nick Hayek, CEO of Swatch, said turnover in Japan was growing at double-digit rates despite the recent abandonment of the franc's euro peg.[18] The types that dropped in absolute terms were textiles and clothing; leather, rubber and plastics; machines, appliances and electronics (very slightly); and precious metals and gemstones. The global recession, Fukushima disaster and Swiss currency volatility may explain these.

JETRO also produced a number of graphs to examine the investment consequences of the deal:

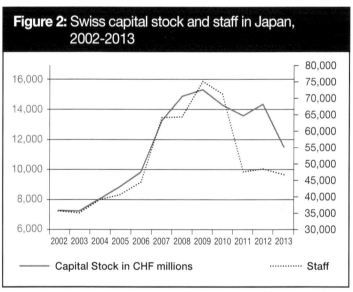

Figure 2: Swiss capital stock and staff in Japan, 2002-2013

Capital Stock in CHF millions ·········· Staff

Source: JETRO 2014

Foreign direct investment is a particularly unpredictable economic indicator, as Michael Burrage has shown.[19] Since investment grew from 2003 and the sharp upward spike began in 2006, the Swiss-Japanese deal cannot really be identified as the cause of this fluctuation, although it is possible that Japanese investors made decisions in 2007-8 with the extra confidence that negotiations were under way. The 2010-13 tailing off may be related to the increased strength of the Swiss franc, as noted in an article in the Neue Zürcher Zeitung: 'That the yen has weakened by about one-fifth since the Abe government took office hampered Swiss exporters'.[20]

However, the comparable graph for foreign direct investment activity in Switzerland is truer to expectation:

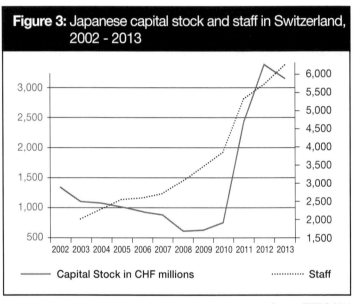

Figure 3: Japanese capital stock and staff in Switzerland, 2002 - 2013

——— Capital Stock in CHF millions ·········· Staff

Source: JETRO 2014

The benefits of the agreement are more evident, or at least more strongly suggested, in this Japanese trade organisation graph. Capital stock in Switzerland seems to have responded directly to the agreement, ending a period of six years' gradual divestment and prompting very rapid investment in the years after it came into force. This went on at the same time the Swiss franc got progressively stronger in the global economy, but did not drop off in 2011 after the euro-peg was introduced. Japanese staffing levels grew throughout the period, indicating that the free movement of business professionals clause was respected by the Swiss, and that the Japanese investment also created jobs for Swiss workers (assuming that otherwise the Japanese staff levels would more closely track the decline, plateau and increase in stock).

The effects of the Swiss-Japanese deal might be further explored in the trade data provided by the Organisation for Economic Cooperation and Development. To partially control for trade fluctuations unrelated to the deal's tariff changes, Japan was compared with a group which saw little tariff changes over the data period

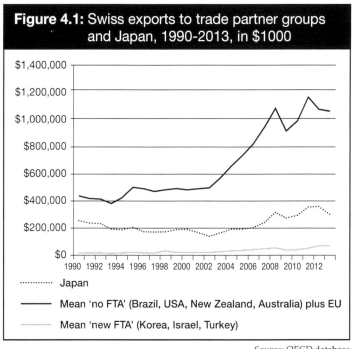

Figure 4.1: Swiss exports to trade partner groups and Japan, 1990-2013, in $1000

.... Japan

———— Mean 'no FTA' (Brazil, USA, New Zealand, Australia) plus EU

———— Mean 'new FTA' (Korea, Israel, Turkey)

Source: OECD database

(i. the EU, with which Switzerland already had a longstanding agreement, and ii. Brazil, America, New Zealand and Australia, with which it has none) and the other countries with which it concluded agreements during the data period (South Korea, Israel, Turkey).

These graphs indicate that the value of imports to Japan does grow, although the trend begins around 2002 and almost plateaus across 2008-2013. The global recession is clearly visible in the Swiss exports to each group, especially that containing the EU, suggesting the minor trough in the Japanese exports line is not unique, but the product of a general Swiss export downturn related to the eurozone crisis and its effect on the Swiss dollar's competitiveness.

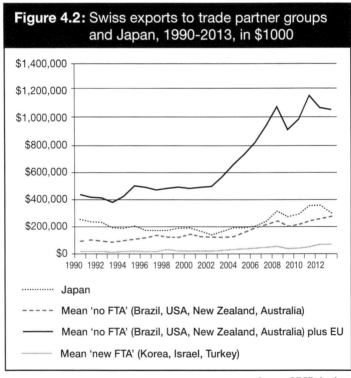

Figure 4.2: Swiss exports to trade partner groups and Japan, 1990-2013, in $1000

.... Japan

- - - - - Mean 'no FTA' (Brazil, USA, New Zealand, Australia)

——— Mean 'no FTA' (Brazil, USA, New Zealand, Australia) plus EU

Mean 'new FTA' (Korea, Israel, Turkey)

Source: OECD database

When Michael Burrage looked at the trade benefits of EU membership in this manner, he found that the Single Market did not have the kind of bounce effect one would expect, either.[21] Cross-border trade simply does not occur as straightforwardly as logic would suppose. Given that the Swiss-Japanese deal was not an immediate eradication of all tariffs, but included gradual tariff reduction in important export areas and complications such as rules of origin, the absence of a clear uptick in Swiss exports after 2009 is not too surprising.

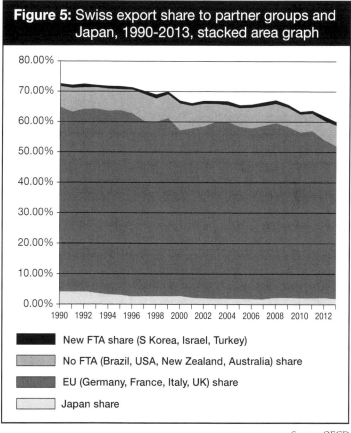

Figure 5: Swiss export share to partner groups and Japan, 1990-2013, stacked area graph

New FTA share (S Korea, Israel, Turkey)

No FTA (Brazil, USA, New Zealand, Australia) share

EU (Germany, France, Italy, UK) share

Japan share

Source: OECD

This graph uses the same groups as above to see whether the Swiss-Japanese deal has instead had an effect on the export share of goods to Japan. Japan's share declines in the 1990s then plateaus from 2004, whereas the EU's declines quite steeply from 2008. The share of the 'No FTA' group also declines in the last few years. This might indicate that the Swiss-Japanese deal allowed Swiss exports to persevere even as Swiss imports grew more to the rest of the world – the white in the graph. This reflects the Swiss position, which sees some agreements as important not in boosting all sales but in defending current trade privileges.

Another way to look at the data is to view Swiss exports to the different groups as percentages of their exports in 2008, the year before the deal came into force.

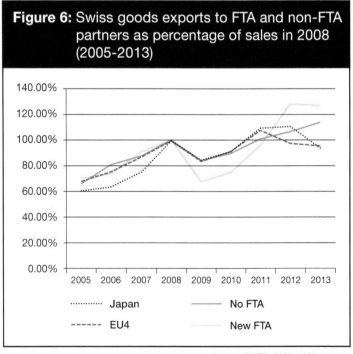

Figure 6: Swiss goods exports to FTA and non-FTA partners as percentage of sales in 2008 (2005-2013)

Source: OECD, 2008 = 100 per cent

This graph primarily demonstrates quite how much the financial crisis affects the evaluation. The other new Swiss trade deal countries' exports recovered sharpest after the sharpest fall, which is good news for the Swiss economics secretariat and indicates that these newer markets are more elastic. Japanese sales were affected very similarly to those of EU, possibly suggesting the depth of all the Single Market rules that Switzerland participates in through the bilaterals does not differ markedly from a comprehensive free trade agreement.

The clearest evidence of the positive impact of the trade and economic partnership comes from a recent analysis from the University of Zurich that uses a different methodology.[22] The authors specifically compare the growth of Swiss goods exports to Japan that were newly liberalised (LG) by the trade and economic partnership, compared to non-liberalised goods (NLG) – those which were already liberalised through the World Trade Organisation processes, or not covered by trade and economic partnership. This method should control better for external factors such as exchange rates, transport costs, market confidence and so on, all of which affect general Swiss-Japanese trade at the exact same time as the trade and economic partnership came into effect. Comparing LG with NLG goods still requires the assumption that external shocks affect the two categories of goods equally, but this is a fair assumption since both sets are quite diverse – NLG in this case includes some agricultural goods (already protected) but also information/communication technology and pharmaceutical products (already liberalised).

The trade and economic partnership macro analysis found that there was 'a statistically significant positive effect on Swiss exports to Japan already during the first year after [the FTA] becoming effective [sic]' in the value-weighted growth rates of liberalised goods.[23] Data was only available up until 2010, but shows clearly that the trade and economic partnership did have an effect on Swiss exports 'significantly different from zero'.[24] Japanese liberalised exports did not, in fact, fare so well over the period. It must be remembered that over these years, use of the deal's preferential rates was only 24–50 per cent, so the full potential of the agreement was far from being reached.

The Zurich economists conclude that the trade deal was 'a success story' based on the 15 months after the deal came into force. They were looking at short-term effects, but recall that both nations' negotiating teams had always held 'the firm conviction that the true benefits of free trade agreements do materialize *in the long run*' as the most competitive companies and locations gradually win out.[25] This strongly suggests that the economic benefits of the deal are only just emerging.

Business activity

There have been several interesting developments in the business interactions of Swiss and Japanese firms since the deal's signing. Although it is hard to tell whether or not they would have happened without the treaty, they may give a flavour of the current commercial relationship.

Reviewing the impact of the deal in 2010, Michiaki Watanabe of the Japanese external trade body noted that many other Japanese businesses had recently set up in Switzerland:

Sunstar
Nissan
Elpida Memory

Tillot Pharma (Zeria Pharma)
Toyota Textile Machinery
Summit minerals (Sumitomo Corp)
Allied Telesis
Hirotech
MS Frontier Reinsurance (Mitsui Sumitomo Insurance)
Quadrant (Mitsubishi Plastics)
Shiseido
Namiki
Tokio Millennium Reinsurance (Tokyo Marine & Nichido Fire Insurance)
VS Technology[26]

This is an impressive list, especially given that the presentation was delivered just a year after the deal came into force. These cannot all be attributed to the deal coming into force, but the link is heavily suggested by the Japanese external trade organisation. Other examples include:

Electricity distribution partnership

The Japanese giant Hitachi and Swiss firm ABB agreed in 2014 to supply Japan with electric power grid equipment through a new joint venture. This follows attempts by Shinzo Abe's government to liberalise the energy market, which is currently uncompetitive due to local monopolies. The partnership will be Tokyo-based and 51 per cent owned by Hitachi, but will use ABB's high voltage direct current technology.[27]

Swiss chocolate in Japan

In 2013 the Swiss chocolatier Barry Callebaut opened an 18 million franc factory in Takasaki, Gunma Prefecture, north-west of Tokyo. The Japanese chocolate market is worth over $11 billion. Barry Callebaut already had an alliance with Morinaga & Co., a sweet company, and aims to expand.[28]

Cloud robotics

Rapyuta Robotics, a start-up founded by two Sri Lankans in Tokyo, aims to create a cloud infrastructure for robots to share their learning experiences and learn from one another. Their initial products may include drones for security and infrastructure inspection in bridges and tunnels. One founder and several of the team were trained in Zurich and the technical side of the start-up is stationed in Switzerland, the investment side and planned drone use in Japan. The company raised nearly $3 million in seed funding before even producing a prototype.[29]

Another cloud start-up, Midokura, set up its European headquarters in Renens, then moved to Lausanne.[30]

Pharmaceutical buy-outs

Takeda Pharmaceutical Company announced it would take over Nycomed in summer 2011 for 9.6 billion euros. Nycomed was originally a Norwegian pharmaceutical, but had been (and continues to be) based in Zurich. Takeda was already strong in Japan and America but bought Nycomed thanks to its European and emerging market presence.[31]

Cosmetics

Swiss cosmetics made noteworthy gains in Japan, particularly anti-aging products producer Valmont and proactive firms Lydia Dainow, Celicosmet and Paul Scerri.[32]

Architectural cooperation

There are several examples of Japanese architects working in Switzerland. These included the Rolex Learning Center on the campus of the Swiss Federal Institute of Technology, Lausanne, which opened in 2010, and commissions to construct both headquarters for Swatch and a new production building for Omega from the architect of the Tamedia New Office Building, which opened in Zurich in 2013. The Circle at Zurich Airport is to open in 2018.[33]

Smart grid technology

Toshiba Corporation bought the smart grid tech firm Landis + Gyr, from Zug Canton, in 2011 for $2.3 billion as part of its strategy to diversify from energy generation equipment to distribution. Paul Peyrot, executive director of the Swiss Chamber of Commerce, thought the purchase was based on Landis + Gyr having a very strong market position.[34] It already exported over 72,000 units to Finland and China, and in 2015 won a contract for 36,000 more to sell to Poland's distribution operators. It remains an independent growth platform for Toshiba.[35]

It is apparent that Switzerland negotiated a beneficial deal with Japan in 2009 despite being a smaller economy and not being part of a trading bloc like the EU. Part of Switzerland's attraction was its access to the EU's Single Market but it was also important as a market in itself, and for geostrategic reasons. The trade deal reduced tariffs on iconic Swiss food products and improved conditions for the sale of services and investment. Switzerland also gained diplomatic access to Japan that resulted in several other agreements. The economic impact of the deal indicates that although there is still scope for improved use of the deal, Swiss goods have benefitted in the years since the deal came into force.

Part 2

Lessons for Britain

5

How comparable are Switzerland and Britain?

If Britain left the EU it would be in a situation it has not been in for more than 40 years: controlling its own trade policy. The global trading situation and Britain's Foreign Office personnel have changed a lot in that time, meaning all lessons from countries already in this new situation will be important. Britain will need to learn how significant continued Single Market access would be, how to set out a negotiation strategy, what pitfalls to avoid and what opportunities to pursue.

The Swiss case study only provides useful lessons for Britain outside the EU if Switzerland's situation is comparable to Britain's. Some may argue that Switzerland is too dissimilar to work as a meaningful comparison, but this is only a tenable position if viable comparisons require such high levels of similarity that almost all economics breaks down.

Other countries that might be used as comparisons have more differences to Britain. America is too large economically, Canada is too rich in natural resources, Japan is too far away, Norway has too much oil and salmon, Algeria has oil and is mostly desert, Turkey is both too industrial and too agricultural. Every comparison can be dismissed.

In fact, Switzerland offers the best proxy one could reasonably hope for. Both countries have unusually large financial services sectors and strong tourism sectors. Both control their own currencies and have central banks independent of government. Whilst Switzerland's population is smaller than Britain's, it has a similar population density and distribution.[1]

Switzerland's export profile is notably similar to Britain's. As the charts derived from OEC data show, both the goods the two countries export, and their destinations, are similar.[2]

Both countries' exports show extremely mixed economies, but even their key export industries are similar. The machines product type features largely in both (21.33 per cent from Britain, 14.8 per cent from Switzerland), as do precious metals (5.44 per cent to 25.13 per cent) and chemical products (15.99 per cent to 25.13 per cent). Of course the two are not identical – the Swiss sell more watches, gold and jewellery, while Britain sells far more cars and oil. Nevertheless, these profiles are much more similar to one another than Britain is to most developed countries, and certainly enough to make broad arguments on trade policy.

Switzerland and Britain have a similar mix of export partners, selling mostly to nearby European states and around 10 per cent to the US, and very little to Africa, Australasia or South America. The main difference, that Switzerland exports proportionally more to Asian countries, underlines Switzerland's success in embracing global trade. Even without a free trade deal its exports to India (10.6 per cent) are proportionally much greater than Britain's (1.54 per cent) despite the absence of Swiss post-colonial links there. Hong Kong,

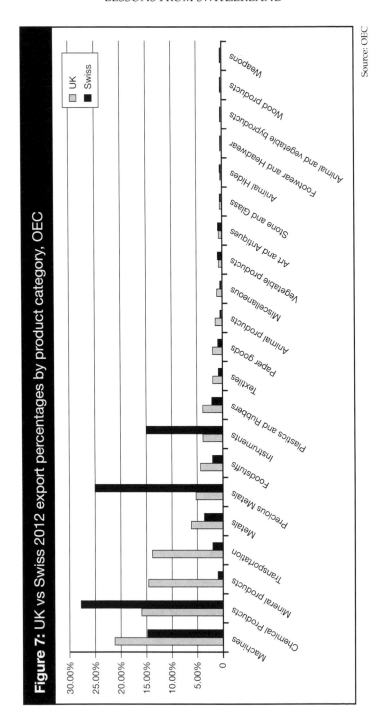

Figure 7: UK vs Swiss 2012 export percentages by product category, OEC

Source: OEC

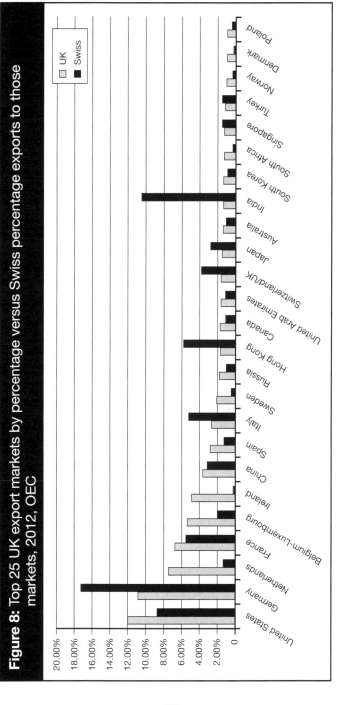

Figure 8: Top 25 UK export markets by percentage versus Swiss percentage exports to those markets, 2012, OEC

Source: OEC

Japan and Singapore all feature more prominently as export destinations for Switzerland. The UK sells slightly more to northwest Europe and Ireland, while Switzerland is closer to its neighbours Germany and Italy. Again, these export destinations show Switzerland is the closest viable UK proxy, and closer than the other often-raised Brexit examples like Norway, Turkey, Greenland, Iceland or Mexico.

An important advantage the Swiss had was that they were not perceived as a major threat to Japanese agriculture. Only 1.4 per cent of sales to Japan were agricultural. The Japanese agricultural ministry was using the Swiss deal to show that it was willing to compromise and liberalise food markets to some extent. This meant Switzerland's size, far smaller than the US or the EU, was actually an advantage because Swiss farm exports were not a danger to Japanese farmers. The UK's food exports to Japan are similarly small, an average of 3.83 per cent of total exports from 2010-2012 counting foodstuffs or 5.52 per cent including foodstuffs, vegetable products, food byproducts, and animal products.[3]

Reducing tariffs on British food products would then be a larger concession for the Japanese, so this might be an area in which British negotiators have to consider limiting their tariff reduction ambitions for the good of the wider process. Diplomats could certainly liberalise specific mutual interests such as whisky. Considering Britain's trade prospects more generally, Figure 7 shows that food and agricultural products make up a relatively small proportion of total British exports, so like Switzerland, Britain should generally come across as unthreatening to states with sensitive farming sectors.

6

The importance of Single Market access

While Switzerland is the chosen case study for its relationship with Japan, the lessons of the Swiss-Japanese deal would apply to Britain without Britain adopting the specific Swiss bilaterals model after an Out referendum vote. Indeed, the Swiss model has a number of drawbacks and tensions with the EU which the UK government would probably try to avoid. This paper simply operates on the assumption that the UK's position outside the EU would be roughly analogous, in that the UK would be outside the EU customs union and EU trade policy, so able to negotiate its own free trade deals independently, but that as a former member and nearby country, the UK would have privileged access to the Single Market. This may well involve monetary contribution and adoption of some percentage of Single Market regulations and directives. Non-European countries considering free trade deals with an independent Britain would not see much difference between a Swiss model, a Norwegian/Icelandic model, or a deep and comprehensive EU-UK free trade agreement: all include privileged access for Britain in the Single Market.

Numerous other publications consider in more detail the possible tactics required to bring Britain to such a situation. In *The Norwegian Way* I argued that adopting a trading relationship similar to Norway's would be simplest after a referendum, since the four Single Market freedoms of goods, capital, labour and services would be retained and there is already a formal structure for updating the agreement, so the EU is least likely to oppose this arrangement.[1] In *With Friends Like These...Why Britain should leave the EU – and how*, David Conway argues that Britain's best gambit for securing a better new relationship with the EU would be to take advantage of the Greek crisis, which he considers likely to force Germany into pushing for a new consolidated treaty. He argues that in exchange for supporting eurozone integration in this treaty, Britain could demand EU acceptance of a separate treaty granting Britain an improved version of the Norwegian relationship.[2] Other arguments rest on mutual self-interest – Britain and the rest of the EU currently trade large volumes with one another with no tariffs, and it is in the interest of exporters from both sides that British exit does not raise barriers. The eurozone economies appear to be fragile enough at present, without worrying about tariff and non-tariff barriers being raised by a major export destination.

Nevertheless, preferential Single Market access cannot be guaranteed. Conway highlights how some remaining EU members are likely to be unwilling to grant Britain an easy ride since Britain flourishing after exit might encourage the dissolution of the union. Under either of the models above, all 27 remaining EU members would have the ability to veto a prospective UK exit arrangement, as well as the three non-EU EEA countries: Iceland, Norway and Liechtenstein. One or several central or eastern member states might veto a deal if it did not grant their nationals' continued migration rights or include continued British contributions to structural funding, for example. Iceland or Norway might veto a treaty that gave Britain a better deal than theirs, as Conway's gambit proposes. Moreover, the eurozone countries might develop a model of integration that did not require British support, just as the Fiscal Compact went ahead despite David Cameron's veto. Senior European politicians like Sigmar Gabriel and Emmanuel Macron may be planning to pursue eurozone integration through the enhanced cooperation mechanism of the Lisbon Treaty, which would not require treaty change or British support. Equally, if there was a treaty conference, Greece or Spain might resist the integration treaty as a further loss of sovereignty, ruining the British side of the deal in passing. In any case, no serious movement on the issue is likely to come about until after the French and German 2017 elections, at which point Britain will have already had its referendum or be about to vote.

Just as negotiating a trade deal with Japan would require substantial concessions and committed negotiation from Britain, so too would retaining preferential EU Single Market access or membership in the event of an Out vote. The possibility that preferential Single Market access might not be lost has an impact on the value of Switzerland as a case study. Of course, the comparison requires other assumptions: that the UK does not break apart due to Scottish withdrawal following the referendum, that the economy remains in roughly the structure it exhibits now, that Britain's United Nations and Nato memberships continue. This scenario does not consider whether Britain would cut a great deal of EU-related product and labour regulations (red tape) after exit, which might make it more attractive and competitive. Such regulatory changes would partly depend on the specific form of post-exit EU relationship, and partly on the will of the British public.

It is difficult to fully address the counterfactual question, 'Would the Swiss-Japanese deal have gone ahead without Swiss preferential access to the Single Market?' Certainly, the anonymous Japanese Foreign Ministry official who spoke to the *Japan Times* seemed to value Switzerland's being in Europe, but did not go on to specify the importance of the Single Market itself. The Japanese elite viewed Switzerland as a modest prospect in itself, but an important step in acclimatising the sensitive fishing, agricultural and industrial sectors to a trade deal with an economically advanced European country.

The Japanese were worried that three trade blocs were developing, based around the Americas, Europe and North Africa and east Asia. Although themselves part of the east Asian bloc, they considered this three-bloc future a threat to world trade since Japanese exports to America and Europe were also very important. They saw a deal with Switzerland as a means of connecting with Europe to counterbalance the EU's tendency to focus on its own bloc.[3] This does not mean simply that Switzerland would be a bridge for selling Japanese goods to the EU. The rules of origin exist to stop this kind of third country trade – if they did not, then Japan would be equally exposed to tariff-free EU goods sold to it through Switzerland. If that was Japan's intent then it would have simply prioritised a trade deal with the

EU itself.

The advantage for Japanese goods in terms of selling to the EU is only evident in the case of subsidiaries. The deal makes it easier for Japanese investors to set up businesses or subsidiaries in Switzerland. These subsidiaries, if they were selling goods which met EU rules of origin, could sell into the EU Single Market tariff free because they would be originating in Switzerland. This is not an advantage to be dismissed, but equally does not seem to be the centrepiece of the deal.

The conclusion seems to be rather that in 2009 Japan was making a number of deals with medium sized states as experiments to show sensitive domestic sectors that such deals were not a major threat, and could be beneficial to the country. Access to the Single Market is not the only reason Japan signs trade agreements with countries that are small like Switzerland. In the last decade it has signed agreements with Chile and Peru. It has also signed an important deal with Australia, which came into force in January 2015. Australia is roughly half the size of Britain economically, and has also signed trade deals with China and South Korea in recent years.

A brief look at the Australian deal shows that major economies such as Japan are willing to grant significant tariff concessions to states that are neither as large as the EU or US, nor have privileged access to them. This is especially noteworthy since one of Australia's export strengths is in food and drink products, precisely those that Japanese institutions are historically protective of. Yet the Australian-Japanese deal eliminated the tariff on bulk wine and phases out the 15 per cent tariff on bottled wine over seven years, apparently already having boosted sales value by 17 per cent compared to the same quarter of 2014.[4] The deal also gave Australian beef farmers a 7 per cent tariff advantage against competitors like America.[5] This advantage will grow to 15 per cent incrementally.[6]

In exchange, Australia reduced tariffs on Japanese cars, household appliances and clothing – which its prime minister, Tony Abbott, celebrated as a saving to the Australian consumer. Notably, Australian negotiators achieved this while keeping any mention of investor-state dispute settlement mechanisms out of the deal with Japan.[7]

This recent Australian example illustrates that Single Market membership is not necessary for medium economies to forge preferential trading relationships with large economies. In sum, it would certainly help Britain's trading prospects with the rest of the world to have privileged access to the EU Single Market, but failing to do so would not be a serious setback.

Therefore the Swiss case study can be used as a model for the UK's trade policy outside the EU, from which the UK government can learn important lessons on conducting future negotiations.

7

What can Britain learn?

The need for an experienced team of trade negotiators

Negotiation difficulties arise when the different departments of a country's government contradict one another on negotiation priorities, with no clear leadership.

Before starting any detailed talks with a prospective partner, the British government should conduct a comprehensive private review of the opportunities the potential trade alliance offers, and the sectors at risk, and internally agree on absolute red lines, as well as areas which are desirable but can be conceded if required. The government should also clearly assign a department to coordinate and represent the UK effort (probably the Foreign Office), along with a prominent cabinet minister as free trade agreement tsar, the visible spokesperson for the negotiation. A public consultation should also be carried out. This would allow better transparency and communication with the public during the talks, and would be important for selling the eventual deal to the public and to parliament when concluded, in the manner Cecilia Malmström is attempting somewhat retroactively for the EU in the case of the Transatlantic Trade and Investment Partnership.

Since the EU has been in charge of negotiating free trade agreements on behalf of Britain for so long, the UK may not have the staff, experience or expertise to represent itself on the world stage, especially if it is to conduct exit negotiations from the EU and be an active participant in the top-table international bodies like the WTO and UN Economic Commission for Europe at the same time. This may be a reasonable concern – the Foreign Office would certainly need a recruitment drive and funding boost in the event of Brexit.[1] The Swiss-Japanese deal took six years to negotiate from the initial joint feasibility studies to entry into force: it would be important that Britain tries not to take longer than this with its first post-Brexit deals so it does not fall behind other developed countries. However, Britain does have a team of negotiators – the government can and does still conduct bilateral investment talks and treaties,[2] plus those who currently represent Britain in the EU, and of course has negotiators in non-economic roles.

The problem is far from insuperable, especially as far as trade agreements are concerned. There is no reason why Britain could not recruit experienced negotiators from other states that have a proven free trade agreement track record, such as Australia, New Zealand, Canada, Norway, and of course Switzerland. As mentioned already, Australia alone has recently concluded trade deals with South Korea, China and Japan. British politics has a healthy recent history of hiring experts from the Anglophone world, from Lynton Crosby to Ryan Coetzee to Dame Lowell Goddard. Hiring veteran negotiators from small and medium sized countries that have already concluded significant trade deals is a logical step.

Indeed, many such diplomats may have the interpersonal relationships or contacts that make negotiations that bit faster and smoother. EU negotiators do not always have such soft power advantages, not having concluded agreements with so many countries. Australia's trade deal with Japan includes preferential tariffs for beef, prawns, lobster, asparagus and other Australian goods, proving that Switzerland is not unique as a small country successfully negotiating its way into much larger markets.[3]

Concessions

The mood in Japan during the Swiss-Japanese deal's negotiation is interesting to compare with the tone of the European Commission's draft inception report on an EU-Japan comprehensive trade and investment agreement. We can see then what the EC was considering conceding on Britain's behalf, and how the UK might benefit. The two together point towards the kinds of areas an independent Britain should consider.

Most of the EU summary does not even talk about economics, but emphasises potential social and environmental effects.[4] In its detail, the Commission document does discuss addressing non-tariff measures (technical barriers to trade) and how they could be reduced for financial services, distribution, railway equipment, automobiles, machinery and pharmaceuticals.[5] Elsewhere, the Commission notes that:

> The sectors with the largest potential increase of EU exports as a result of NTM [non-tariff measure] reduction are the motor vehicle sector, the pharmaceutical and the transport equipment sectors. Concerning the services sectors, there is

also a potential to reduce barriers, especially in the finance and telecommunication sectors.[6]

The document goes on to forecast the potential cost reductions that removing non-tariff measures could bring to these sectors:

Table 2: Degree of potential NTM reduction in Japan & resulting EU export increase for key sectors

Sector	Cost of existing NTMs as barriers to trade (AVE, %)	Potential reduction of NTMs (% points)	Export increase for the EU (billion Euros)
Motor Vehicles	10	7	4.7
Pharmaceutical	22	20	3.4
Medical Devices	30	12	1.1
Processed foods	25	9	1
Transport equipment (railway equipment and aircraft)	45	40	2.6 (aircraft 2; railway equipment 0.6)
Finance	15.8	8.7	Not available (total EU exports to Japan: 2.2)
Insurance	6.5	1.2	Not available
Business and ICT	2.5	2.5	Not available
Communications	24.7	19.2	Not available (total EU exports to Japan: 3.3)
Contruction	2.5	1.9	Not available
Personal, cultural, other services	6.5	3.7	Not available

Source: European Commission, 'Trade Sustainability Impact Assessment', Draft Inception Report, (January 2015), p.38

These priority sectors are actually all areas in which Britain could do well, so at first glance, the Commission is thinking along the right lines.[7] However, when you consider other factors, the prospects of such a deal really helping the UK wane and wane. Firstly, France is likely to require a cultural exemption similar to that of TTIP, meaning potential gains in telecommunications are limited. Secondly, none of the EC or European Parliament's work on the financial sector in the last three years has indicated sympathy for the City or an intention to help reduce barriers. Finally, very few people in the EU or media are talking seriously about concluding a Japanese deal. TTIP is already behind schedule and a great deal of EU activity is introspective, considering how to deal with Greece and the eurozone crisis and how to accommodate Britain's renegotiation ambitions. If an EU-Japan free trade agreement is on the horizon, then it is extremely distant and indistinct.

What the Commission document actually demonstrates, then, is that there are great potential benefits for members from an FTA with Japan, if the will to conclude one was actually there. With greater emphasis on the specific sectors in which Britain specifically can flourish, a bilateral free trade agreement appears to be a more realistic prospect.

This impression is confirmed by another table in the same document, which looks at which sectors have already been mentioned in the early and preparatory stages of negotiations (a scoping exercise, and illustrative roadmap, and impact assessment report, and feedback from the European Parliament and Commission). Financial services were mentioned only in the scoping exercise.[8] Britain alone would be much more likely to prioritise greater access to the City of London.

A Japan-EU trade deal remains very unlikely according to Ziltener and Chiavacci, certainly at the level of depth Britain could achieve in a bilateral deal.[9] As Japanese trade with Switzerland remains low as a proportion of Japan's total international trade, it is very possible that Japan would be open to the prospect of another free trade agreement with a second European economy. The UK, as a G8 economy and sizeable market in itself, already host to several important Japanese businesses, should be an attractive prospect. But what offers could British negotiators make?

Japanese negotiations with the EU are technically open but virtually static. Britain is considerably larger than Switzerland, so less low-risk, low-return, but compared to the EU, whose combined economy is greater than that of any country including the US, Britain cannot be considered daunting. To put it simply, Britain would probably be seen as medium-risk, medium-return.

By being energetic in pursuit of trade deals, Britain could act as a European bulkhead for a number of other important states which have yet to sign deals with either Switzerland or the EU: Australia, Brazil, India and Indonesia. Brazil might be an especially important deal in the future as it is currently locked out of the Trans Pacific Partnership and TTIP so needs economic friends outside Latin America. Along with India, it is also a nation considered to have high long-term prospects.[10] As discussed earlier, Britain signing free trade deals with countries before the EU does the same would mean those countries are more likely to build subsidiaries in Britain, to take advantage both of its own market and its proximity to Europe and privileged access. Britain is already seen as welcoming to international investment, but depending on public consensus, could be an even more attractive prospect if it embraced investor protection clauses like the contentious chapter of TTIP, or reduced internal regulation.

We know that Swiss negotiators were happy to reduce tariffs on key Japanese exports in the course of their deal's negotiation. By inheriting the current system of EU external tariffs, Britain would have some important product areas in which to grant concessions such as automobiles, agricultural and fisheries products, aluminium, and tobacco products. The UK also has a lot to offer in terms of procurement and private contracting, business services, and privileged movement for business people. Of course, some of these might be sensitive areas that the public or UK business wish to protect, but arguably such concessions are better decided at a national level. In this manner, the UK could get the tariff and regulatory advantages on certain goods and services, with which it would then be likely to outcompete the remaining EU. The idea that Britain would have no meaningful bargaining chips because it would already be an open economy is inaccurate. Indeed, Switzerland is generally regarded as a very open economy but still has areas where it can grant concessions in return to better access with privileged partners.

We have seen that the Swiss deal also covers movement rights, allowing business people to travel between the signatory nations temporarily. This element is seen in most modern trade deals, since it facilitates investment and the spread of knowledge and skills. Although it is a much more restrictive proposal than the EU's free movement of people, such a clause in a free trade deal may still be unwelcome to British voters, as it would contribute to overall annual immigration figures. With Japan that might not be a large problem, but it could be more contentious if the same clause was included in free trade deals with populous states like India, China or Brazil. Of course such a clause would not be fundamental to most deals, but if Britain refused that kind of clause it might be expected to grant greater concessions in other areas, like sensitive tariffs or services. Indeed, there are rumours that disagreement over skilled temporary migration caused the current deadlock in the EU-India free trade discussions. After the EU referendum, the British public will need to have a transparent debate about what levels of immigration and integration it favours, and how highly population control is valued compared to optimising trade agreements.

Global strategy

The Swiss government does not see individual trade deals in isolation. Its priorities are often reacting to, or pre-empting, privileged trade agreements between major powers so it can stay with or ahead of the global pack. While Britain is currently in this pack as an EU member, it will need to follow the Swiss example and commit to a long-term strategy of trade and investment partnerships if it leaves the EU. This is important, not only in straightforward tariff and quota terms, but to have a say over global trading rules.

Failing to play a leading role in global regulation and standards setting bodies could leave the UK slightly disadvantaged compared to EU members. Interacting with the world regulatory systems as energetically as Switzerland and Norway do will be equally important for the UK, since the EU is our largest market (if taken collectively).[11] Not doing so could leave the UK reacting to EU rules and applying them to most of the economy without much contribution to their drafting, just as sceptics complain Britain does now.

This is because inadequate contribution to the WTO, UN, Basel Commission, Organisation for Economic

Cooperation and Development, and other bodies could leave Britain exposed to the 'Brussels effect', a regulatory pattern first described by Anu Bradford of Columbia Law School.[12] Bradford (and later Chad Damrod) showed that the EU had worldwide influence in product areas in which it was the first to produce tight regulations, such as air safety and anti-trust law.[13] This is because, once the EU produces regulations for what a company can sell into the Single Market, non-EU exporters are incentivised to adapt their processes to conform to those regulations, so those non-EU exporters' host countries more or less follow legislative suit.

Moreover, once a set of trading rules are adopted at the WTO level, they can erode national sovereignty in the same way as aspects of the EU. Likewise other treaties have elements that transcend a signatory's legal system such as upcoming intellectual property and services trade agreements under the WTO umbrella. Nation states have a say on passing or rejecting the original WTO rules, but must submit in cases of conflicting interpretation with other nation states to WTO dispute settlement and rulings, which are binding.

The Brussels effect is likely to be magnified by TTIP as regulatory convergence is a key aim for both American and European sides, meaning that when it is eventually concluded and brought into force, the world's exporters will certainly take notice as they will want their products to be sellable in the two largest global economies. This does not necessarily imply that Britain would be better off as a member state feeding into TTIP, since Britain's individual influence on the Commission's collective negotiating position is diffuse and liable to opposition from EU members with other priorities.

According to UK government representatives, the UK has already contributed to TTIP, so exporters could benefit from the standards agreed even if Britain has to enter the deal as a third party later.[14] Britain would only need to do this for the tariff benefits – broadly speaking the regulatory standardisation is a benefit to all the world's exporters, regardless of TTIP involvement, just as it would help UK exporters now if every Central and South American state adopted US product regulations today. The UK might have more concrete input by helping draft laws at the WTO level, which are merely copied and enshrined in TTIP.

The 1995 General Agreement on Trade in Services (GATS) is a good example of this – it was agreed at the WTO and is now used as a template for services agreements in most free trade deals, the Swiss-Japanese deal included. Joining TTIP as a third party might allow Britain to stay clear of the sections the public would be concerned about, such as possible additional NHS privatisation, allowing genetically-modified and hormone-treated foods into supermarkets, and an investor-state dispute mechanism that may allow multinationals to intimidate governments out of tightening or changing business regulation. This would mean British producers of comparable products would lose tariff-free access to US markets, so would be at a comparative disadvantage with the EU's exporters of those products.

One of the clearest consequences of TTIP will be new rules on endocrine disruptors in pesticides. They are a group of chemicals that can interfere with natural hormones and may be linked to a number of serious health problems. The EU decided to regulate pesticides that act as endocrine disruptors in 2011 but has not yet implemented restrictions because there is internal Commission disagreement over the breadth of the ban.

The EU would normally use a method called the precautionary principle to regulate endocrine disruptors, which would ban any chemicals that could in theory cause harm, but the EU is being lobbied to ban only chemicals about which there is already data of negative effects from exposure. The former approach would ban far more than the latter, so would have a much greater effect on the chemicals industry and the agricultural sector. The US Department of Agriculture is pushing for the latter definition, since the majority of US export crops are treated with pesticides. The EC was supposed to make a decision in December 2013 but still has not (as of July 2015), prompting Sweden and Denmark to file a lawsuit against the Commission. If TTIP accepts the weaker definition, this will have wide ranging implications for Swiss and UK chemical and agricultural producers, as well as consumers, even if Britain were out of the EU. This is because it will directly apply in the EU and US markets, so illustrates Bradford's Brussels effect, where third party producers will choose to conform in order to export, and their governments usually legislate accordingly.

On the other side of the world, Japan is currently involved in negotiating the Trans-Pacific Partnership (TPP), a multinational free trade and economic agreement led by America. It already has agreements with TPP members Australia, Mexico, Chile, Brunei, Singapore, Vietnam and Peru, and needs to conclude more with Canada and Colombia. The Trans Pacific Partnership is evidently a deal similar to TTIP on the US west coast, and one that UK trade policy should bear in mind because of its potential to multiply the world regulation effect described above. Switzerland's Japanese deal gives it access to a key Trans-Pacific Partnership member, so its exporters will have an incentive to produce goods that meet the regulatory standards of all the partnership's signatories. Britain could do the same – if Britain were already a member of TTIP then its exports would already conform to US rules, so should be close to Pacific partnership rules too.

Together the EU and US will be Britain's key partners in market regulation, so the FCO will need to work extra hard, ally with one or other on important topics, or indeed with Japan or China, to try to get ahead of the game. Together the US and Europe are about 66.45 per cent of our goods export market, and pivoting to the developing world cannot be done so quickly as to avoid this fact.[15] While maintaining close Western market access, Switzerland has pre-empted both of those powers in its deals with the largest Asian economies, and the UK would need to act quickly after leaving the EU to achieve the same result.

In considering an EU-Japan trade agreement, the EC itself acknowledged:

> The conclusion of mega regional agreements will also shape international trade and investment governance in a wide range of policy areas, from rules of origin to investment and government procurement. It will therefore be important to assess the degree to which the approach to negotiations of the EU-Japan agreement is compatible with other mega regional agreements, as this will have a bearing of the course of international trade rules.[sic][16]

This will, then, be an ongoing consideration for British interests, whether inside or outside the EU. As explained above, working in the international standards-setting bodies to influence the parameters of future regulation direction, concluding large bilateral deals before the largest powers do, and lobbying the TTIP partners, will be crucial to promoting British interests.

Rules of origin

If the UK left the EU, it would almost certainly benefit in the same manner Switzerland does from the standardisation of rules of origin templates across Europe and the Mediterranean. Not only has the UK already been operating such harmonised rules of origin for years as part of the extant EU free trade agreements (such as with Mexico, South Korea, South Africa) but it will probably need to agree to these agreements on the same terms during EU exit negotiations, so will already be party to many such agreements.

It is also very likely that the same or similar rules of origin will apply to EU-UK trade, assuming the UK negotiates a free trade agreement or deeper set of bilateral trade agreements with the EU during exit. It is very difficult to see why the EU would try to introduce any more stringent rules of origin in an EU-UK free trade agreement, as it would inconvenience EU exporters just as much as British ones, with no advantage in preventing transhipment. Inheriting the standardised rules template that covers Europe and the Mediterranean would initially be useful to UK exporters since they would only need to produce one version of paperwork to show their products were eligible for free trade agreement tariff reductions, and their products that were agreement-viable for one free trade partner would usually be viable for all other free trade partners.

Mexico and India are large countries which can get their own way in setting homogenous rules of origin across multiple free trade agreements (unlike Chile, New Zealand or Singapore). In the longer term this indicates that Britain, with a larger economy than either, could have an important role to play in setting rules of origin, following the EU's old templates but modernising them in trade agreements it concludes with states before the EU.

In addition, the evidence of slow uptake of the Swiss-Japanese deal by Swiss exporters presents important lessons for UK governments negotiating their own trade agreements in the future, or even considering how to optimise EU-led trade agreements. The initial fixed costs of understanding and conforming to rules of origin must be overcome for a company to benefit from an agreement, however deep and comprehensive it is. Small and medium sized businesses that might be wary of such hurdles, or unaware of how to approach them, should receive attention from the Department for Business, Innovation and Skills, ideally before an agreement even comes into force so they have plenty of time to consider and adapt. This attention should include clear advice on the government's website, training or seminars, and perhaps even small business loans targeted to boost the agreement's uptake by meeting the initial fixed costs.

Greater potential for use of free trade in foreign policy

An advantage of conducting trade in a Swiss manner is that Britain would be freer to use trade policy as a wing of foreign policy. As an example, at the time of writing (July 2015), the West's relations with Iran are tentatively warming as leaders come to an agreement on nuclear power. If this improvement continues, an independent Britain could lead the way in ending the boycott and opening free trade talks (within the provisos of international agreements). Iran is, even despite years of being shut out of the wealthiest countries' markets, about as economically important as Norway or Austria, with a large population and rich culture.[17] Such a deal would be virtually impossible from within the EU, where any member state could have reservations and veto talks, so the example illustrates that the wider possibilities of an independent trade policy go beyond strict economic concerns.

We saw in Part One that Swiss ministers gained a great deal of high level access to their Japanese counterparts as a result of the trade deal and its review clauses. This is an important potential benefit that does not seem to be reflected in Britain's current trade agreements. British ministers and officials do not appear to get such high level treatment from the EU's FTA partners – although Vince Cable did receive delegations from both Mexico and Korea during his tenure as business secretary. Cable's meetings pale in comparison to the closer Swiss-Japanese relationship, which yielded other progress not strictly included in the agreement.

In 2014, Prime Minister Shinzo Abe of Japan and President Didier Burkhalter of Switzerland met in Tokyo to observe the signing of a new open skies agreement to allow airlines from either country to set flight routes and determine the volume of flights freely. This should intensify competition and reduce air fares, with dynamic impact on tourism and business travel between the two. The premiers also discussed acting as intermediaries in other countries' trade disputes, and concerns over security.[18]

This underlines the enhanced top-table access the Swiss-Japanese deal seems to have delivered to Switzerland, which does not seem like an insignificant minnow in the world stage, as some fear Brexit would deliver Britain.

Conclusion

This study has considered Britain's global trading prospects if it left the EU, using Switzerland as the most similar non-EU country to develop a case study. There are indications that Britain could have a successful independent free trade policy and conclude agreements with the world's largest economies. This would not be simple or automatic, and comes with risks as well as opportunities.

If the difficulties are overcome, the case study implies that Britain could benefit from trade deals by boosting exports, attracting more investment and forging lasting diplomatic links with important partners. By representing itself rather than being one of 28 jostling partners, Britain could focus on winning tariff concessions for its own goods and granting them where the government considers appropriate. Independent control of trade policy would also give Britain more options to use trade as a diplomatic tool.

Expectations should be tempered. The case study shows real Swiss success, not a fairytale deal wherein the small European country won everything it wanted. The Japanese could have dropped their tariffs on Swiss products further, and the EU's supporters may argue that Japan would have surrendered more in a deal with the Commission. This is immaterial – the EU has not concluded a deal with Japan and does not look likely to. At present then, Swiss goods and services have considerable competitive advantage over those of EU member states, including Britain's.

There are several lessons that a post-exit British government should seriously consider following if it is to emulate Switzerland's success. The departments of Whitehall will need to have a unified set of goals and red lines for each negotiation, agreed before talks commence, coordinated by a cabinet level trade tsar. The government must have consulted the British public and businesses to determine an acceptable level of trade protection, including openness to foreign products, investor protection, regulation and migration. Public reluctance to open some of these areas would naturally limit how comprehensive trade deals could be.

Britain would need to contribute energetically to the global bodies that set many of the world's trade rules, so should consider hiring veteran foreign negotiators to boost the number of available diplomats. Failure to do so could leave Britain following most EU and American rules with little influence on them. Experienced staff should also help conclude trade agreements as fast as possible after exit – the Swiss deal took roughly six years from inception to fruition. Once Britain starts concluding such deals, it also needs to focus internally on supporting small businesses navigating the paperwork needed to take advantage of them fully.

Continued British access to the Single Market would be an important attraction for prospective trade partners. It would mean they could build subsidiaries in Britain and sell tariff-free to the EU. However, this was not Switzerland's only attraction to Japan, another important element being that individual states like Britain or Switzerland do not threaten partner countries' sensitive industries in the way the huge EU bloc does.

Japan's and China's willingness to sign free trade deals with Australia show that smaller independent countries can land major agreements despite having no privileged Single Market access.

If Britain voted to leave the EU in 2016 or 2017 the country would face new challenges as it regained full responsibility for representing itself on the world stage. It would not automatically win all the trade deals our exporters would like, or win them as swiftly as might be hoped. The Swiss example suggests, though, that a committed negotiating team from a country much smaller than Britain can make its mark on global trade. By constructing policy on the Swiss example, Britain can be confident that serious talks would yield serious deals.

Notes

Introduction

1   The total list of FTAs is mightily impressive, as demonstrated on the Swiss Secretariat for Economic Affairs (SECO) website: http://www.seco.admin.ch/themen/00513/00515/01330/04619/index.html?lang=en

2   Lindsell, J., 'The Norwegian Way: A case study for Britain's future relationship with the EU', London: Civitas, 2015, pp.13-22: http://www.civitas.org.uk/europe/TheNorwegianWay

3   'Entry into force of the Agreement on Free Trade and Economic Partnership between Japan and the Swiss Confederation and the first meeting of the Joint Committee', Ministry of Foreign Affairs of Japan: http://www.mofa.go.jp/region/europe/switzerland/agree0909/index.html

4   International Monetary Fund website, 2014 dataset, accessed 2015

5   (Nominal USD) Interestingly, Japanese GDP per capita, when calculated in terms of purchasing power parity, is almost identical to Britain's. (Source: World Bank, accessed May 2015: http://data.worldbank.org/indicator/NY.GDP.PCAP.PP.CD?order=wbapi_data_value_2013+wbapi_data_value+wbapi_data_value-last&sort=desc)

6   Japan is a more relevant comparison than Canada for the simple reason that Britain's cultural and linguistic ties with Canada make a theoretical agreement between them too different to a Swiss-Canadian one, whereas Britain and Switzerland are similarly historically removed from Japan.

Chapter 1

1   The complexity of the EEA relationship, in which Norway is the main EEA-EFTA member, is explored in Lindsell, 'The Norwegian Way'

2   The European Economic Community became the European Union on the signing of the Maastricht Treaty (1992)

3   A full list of Swiss free trade agreements and ongoing negotiations can be found on the SECO website, here: http://www.seco.admin.ch/themen/00513/00515/01330/04619/index.html?lang=en

4   Abt, M., 'The Economic Relevance of Free Trade Agreements with Partners outside the EU', Swiss Secretariat for Economic Affairs SECO, Growth & Competition Policy, 2009, p.1

5   Abt, 'The Economic Relevance of Free Trade Agreements with Partners outside the EU', p.3

6   Burrage, M., *Where's the Insider Advantage? A review of the evidence that withdrawal from the EU would not harm the UK's exports or foreign investment in the UK*, London: Civitas, 2014, pp.56-58: http://www.civitas.org.uk/europe/MichaelBurrageEU. TTIP is sometimes called the Trans-Atlantic Free Trade Agreement (TAFTA)

7   For far more discussion on this, see Lindsell, 'The Norwegian Way', pp.67-68

8   A law firm evaluating the Sino-Swiss deal, Wenfei, showed persuasively that this incentivises Swiss and EU multinationals to base more of their operations in Switzerland, to benefit from the FTA's preferential tariffs.

9   Schaub, M., 'Utilization of Free Trade Agreements by Companies Trading in Goods: Focusing on the Japan-Switzerland Free Trade and Economic Partnership Agreement', University of St. Gallen, Basel-Landschaft, 2012, p.106

10   Schaub, 'Utilization of Free Trade Agreements by Companies Trading in Goods: Focusing on the Japan-Switzerland Free Trade and Economic Partnership Agreement', p.109. The full complexity of ROO is something the UK can probably avoid upon exit if it remains part of the Euro-Med Protocol on Rules of Origin. It creates an area across Europe and the Mediterranean (including Switzerland), it 'operates between the EU and the States of the European Free Trade Association (Iceland, Liechtenstein, Norway and Switzerland) and Turkey and the countries which signed the Barcelona Declaration, namely Algeria, Egypt, Israel, Jordan, Lebanon, Morocco, Syria, Tunisia and the Palestinian Authority of the West Bank and Gaza Strip. Faroe Islands have been added to the system as well.' It helps manufactured products' cumulation of origin by allowing the manufacturer to class materials originating in one member as if it originated in the country of manufacture. See: http://ec.europa.eu/taxation_customs/customs/customs_duties/rules_origin/preferential/article_783_en.htm

11   Mijuk, G., 'Swiss Short-Term Debt Yields in Negative Territory', *Wall Street Journal*, 31 August 2011: http://www.wsj.com/articles/SB10001424053111904199404576540601403370190

12   Wearden, G., 'Switzerland pegs Swiss franc to Euro', *Guardian*, 6 October 2011: http://www.theguardian.com/business/2011/sep/06/switzerland-pegs-swiss-franc-euro

13 'Swiss franc soars as Switzerland abandons euro cap', BBC, 15 January 2015: http://www.bbc.co.uk/news/business-30829917

14 Dhingra, S., Ottaviano, G., and Sampson, T., 'Should we stay or should we go? The economic consequences of leaving the EU', LSE British Politics and Policy, 23 March 2015: http://blogs.lse.ac.uk/politicsandpolicy/should-we-stay-or-should-we-go-the-economic-consequences-of-leaving-the-eu/

15 Springford, J., Tilford, S., and Whyte, P., 'The Economic Consequences of Leaving the EU', Centre for European Reform, June 2014, p.34: http://www.cer.org.uk/sites/default/files/publications/attachments/pdf/2014/report_smc_final_report_june2014-9013.pdf

16 'Sabres sheathed: The EU and China have averted a trade war. Or have they?', *The Economist*, 3 August 2013: http://www.economist.com/news/china/21582581-eu-and-china-have-averted-trade-war-or-have-they-sabres-sheathed

17 'Leaving to be like Switzerland: bad for business, bad for Britain', British Influence, 2014: http://britishinfluence.tumblr.com/post/61007825036/leaving-to-be-like-switzerland-bad-for-business

Chapter 2

1 Chiavacci, D., and Ziltener, P., 'Japanese Perspectives on a Free Trade Agreement / Economic Partnership Agreement (FTA/EPA) with Switzerland', University of Zurich, 2008. In: Asiatische Studien: Zeitschrift der Schweizerischen Asiengesellschaft, Vol. 57, No. 1, pp. 5-41. Quotation from p.1: https://www.academia.edu/1401210/Japanese_Perspectives_on_a_Free_Trade_Agreement_Economic_Partnership_Agreement_FTA_EPA_with_Switzerland

2 Chiavacci and Ziltener, 'Japanese perspective on a free trade agreement/economic partnership agreement (FTA/EOA) with Switzerland', p.6

3 In 2007 Japan already had FTAs with Singapore, Mexico, Brunei, Chile, Malaysia, the Philippines, Thailand and Indonesia. Only those with Malaysia, Mexico and Singapore were in force. Chiavacci and Ziltener, 'Japanese perspective on a free trade agreement/economic partnership agreement (FTA/EOA) with Switzerland', pp.6-7

4 Chiavacci and Ziltener, 'Japanese perspective on a free trade agreement/economic partnership agreement (FTA/EOA) with Switzerland', p.10

Mexican economic data, IMF 2014

5   Chiavacci and Ziltener, 'Japanese perspective on a free trade agreement/economic partnership agreement (FTA/EOA) with Switzerland', pp.13-14

6   Chiavacci and Ziltener, 'Japanese perspective on a free trade agreement/economic partnership agreement (FTA/EPA) with Switzerland', p.20

7   As of May 2015

8   The G10 group has no structural relationship to the more familiar G20 or G8. It is a loose alliance that is concerned with the vulnerability of their own economies from excessive agricultural exports.

9   Negishi, M., and Takahara, K., 'Japan settles for "low-risk, low-return" FTA goals', *Japan Times*, 22 April 2005.

10 Chiavacci and Ziltener, 'Japanese perspective on a free trade agreement/economic partnership agreement (FTA/EPA) with Switzerland', p.30

11 Chiavacci and Ziltener, 'Japanese perspective on a free trade agreement/economic partnership agreement (FTA/EOA) with Switzerland', p.31

12 'Free Trade Agreement (FTA) and Economic Partnership Agreement (EPA)', Ministry of Foreign Affairs of Japan website, Economic Diplomacy section: http://www.mofa.go.jp/policy/economy/fta/

Chapter 3

1   Chiavacci and Ziltener, 'Japanese perspective on a free trade agreement/economic partnership agreement (FTA/EOA) with Switzerland', p.11

2   Chiavacci and Ziltener, 'Japanese perspective on a free trade agreement/economic partnership agreement (FTA/EOA) with Switzerland', p.30

3   Chiavacci and Ziltener, 'Japanese perspective on a free trade agreement/economic partnership agreement (FTA/EOA) with Switzerland', p.13

4   JSFTEPA Chapter 7, Articles 62-63. Most specific rules of origin and tariff detail is to be found in the agreement's annexes, available in English on the Japanese trade ministry website, here: http://www.meti.go.jp/policy/trade_policy/epa/epa_en/ch/

5   'MFN' is the 'Most Favoured Nation' principle maintained by the WTO. This means that the tariffs one WTO member applies to the goods of another must be no better or worse than it applies to any other WTO member. The exceptions are lowering tariffs for

developing world nations, and lowering tariffs for preferential trade agreement partners (which include FTA partners.) MFN is therefore the tariff and quota rate Japan applies to most developed countries' exports, including those of the EU, and of Switzerland before JSFTEPA. Schaub, 'Utilization of Free Trade Agreements by Companies Trading in Goods: Focusing on the Japan-Switzerland Free Trade and Economic Partnership Agreement', p.14

6 Swiss Chamber of Commerce and Industry, JSFTEPA: http://www.sccij.jp/about-sccij/free-trade-and-economic-partnership-agreement-ftepa/

7 Japan's current Most Favoured Nation schedule tariffs were found on the WTO website at: http://tariffdata.wto.org/. The JSFTEPA concessions were found in JSFTEPA, Annex I, pp.121-270 (2009 MFN rates are indicated in the annex)

8 WTO data for Japan's MFN schedule: http://tariffdata.wto.org/TariffList.aspx

9 Watanabe, M., 'Recovering situation and imports from Japan', Zurich, 11 May 2011

10 Swiss Chamber of Commerce and Industry, JSFTEPA: http://www.sccij.jp/about-sccij/free-trade-and-economic-partnership-agreement-ftepa/

11 'The deal with the Japanese is a bright spot for exporters', SwissInfo, 20 February 2009: http://www.swissinfo.ch/eng/deal-with-japanese-a--bright-spot--for-exporters/682664

12 Various articles cover these issues on the Civitas blog, particularly those by Edmund Stubbs and Jonathan Lindsell, see: http://civitas.org.uk/newblog/tag/ttip/

13 Watanabe, M., Jetro Powerpoint, Zurich, 10 November 2010

14 'Federal Councillor Schneider-Ammann on economic mission to Japan', SECO website, 03 July 2014: http://www.seco.admin.ch/aktuell/00277/01164/01980/index.html?lang=en&msg-id=53666

Chapter 4

1 As indicated above, most parts of watches were already exported at 0 per cent tariff, which may explain the level of uptake. Blind, G., and Ziltener, P., 'Free Trade Live: insights from the Switzerland-Japan Free Trade and Economic Partnership Agreement', University of Zurich, 2014, pp.57-58. In: Mottini, Roger. Yearbook 2014, 53-63: http://www.zora.uzh.ch/99072/

2 Blind and Ziltener, 'Free Trade Live', p.61

3 Meier, R., 'Freihandelsabkommen Schweiz-Japan macht sich

bezahlt', Switzerland Global Enterprise, 16 November 2011: http://www.s-ge.com/de/blog/freihandelsabkommen-schweiz-japan-macht-sich-bezahlt

4   Meier, R., 'Fünf Jahre Freihandelsabkommen Schweiz-Japan: Sparbilanz bei den Importen', Switzerland Global Enterprise, Japan, 29 August 2014: http://www.s-ge.com/de/blog/fuenf-jahre-freihandelsabkommen-schweiz-japan-sparbilanz-bei-den-i mporten

5   Meier, 'Freihandelsabkommen Schweiz-Japan macht sich bezahlt'

6   Schaub, 'Utilization of Free Trade Agreements by Companies Trading in Goods: Focusing on the Japan-Switzerland Free Trade and Economic Partnership Agreement', p.109

7   The full complexity of rules of origin is something the UK can probably avoid upon exit if it remains part of the Euro-Med Protocol on Rules of Origin. It creates an area across Europe and the Mediterranean (including Switzerland), it 'operates between the EU and the States of the European Free Trade Association (Iceland, Liechtenstein, Norway and Switzerland) and Turkey and the countries which signed the Barcelona Declaration, namely Algeria, Egypt, Israel, Jordan, Lebanon, Morocco, Syria, Tunisia and the Palestinian Authority of the West Bank and Gaza Strip. Faroe Islands have been added to the system as well.' It helps manufactured products' cumulation of origin by allowing the manufacturer to class materials originating in one member as if it originated in the country of manufacture. See: http://ec.europa.eu/taxation_customs/customs/customs_duties/rules_origin/preferential/article_783_en.htm

8   Schaub, 'Utilization of Free Trade Agreements by Companies Trading in Goods: Focusing on the Japan-Switzerland Free Trade and Economic Partnership Agreement', p.111

9   Schaub, 'Utilization of Free Trade Agreements by Companies Trading in Goods: Focusing on the Japan-Switzerland Free Trade and Economic Partnership Agreement', p.111

10 Brasor, P., and Tsubuku, M., 'The Japan-Swiss EPA means nothing to cheese lovers', *Japan Times*, 23 May 2010: http://blog.japantimes.co.jp/yen-for-living/the-japan-swiss-epa-means-nothing-to-cheese-lovers/.
    Of course, this might just mean that no Swiss cheese exporters have utilised the agreement yet, but this seems unlikely since, unlike complicated multi-part products whose sellers must navigate tricky rules of origin, Swiss cheese is fairly easy to verify. The FTEPA agreed preferential tariff on natural cheeses is a drop from 29.8 per cent to 14.9 per cent, via gradual annual steps over 11 years, so would only have been about 2.2 per cent at the time Brasor and Tsubuku were writing.

11 Meier, 'Freihandelsabkommen Schweiz-Japan macht sich bezahlt'

12 Abt, 'The Economic Relevance of Free Trade Agreements with Partners outside the EU', p.1. Switzerland is also an enthusiastic supporter of the WTO initiative, the Agreement on Government Procurement (GPA). This is a plurilateral agreement adopted by almost all OECD states, meaning public entities purchasing goods, services and offering construction contracts must put these out to tender internationally (above a certain value). SECO notes its success in extending GPA-like procurement terms to non-signatories via its FTA strategy, such as Chile, Colombia and Peru, p.10

13 Meier, 'Fünf Jahre Freihandelsabkommen Schweiz-Japan: Sparbilanz bei den Importen'. Author's translation

14 Abt, 'The Economic Relevance of Free Trade Agreements with Partners outside the EU', pp.5-7

15 Abt, 'The Economic Relevance of Free Trade Agreements with Partners outside the EU', p.7

16 Meier, 'Freihandelsabkommen Schweiz-Japan macht sich bezahlt'

17 WTO tariff database: http://tariffdata.wto.org/TariffList.aspx

18 Baghdjian, A., 'Swiss economy steams on after scrapping of cap on franc', BusinessDay Live, 11 May 2015: http://www.bdlive.co.za/world/europe/2015/05/11/swiss-economy-steams-on-after-scrapping-of-cap-on-franc

19 Burrage, M., 'The EU Effect', London: Civitas, 2014: http://www.civitas.org.uk/pdf/eueffect.pdf

20 Zoll, P., 'Potenzial nicht ausgeschöpft', Tokyo, 9 July 2014, author translation: http://www.nzz.ch/wirtschaft/potenzial-nicht-ausgeschoepft-1.18340180

21 Burrage, *Where's the Insider Advantage?*

22 Blind and Ziltener, 'Free Trade Live: insights from the Switzerland-Japan Free Trade and Economic Partnership Agreement', pp.57-58. In: Mottini, Roger. Yearbook 2014. There are whole papers discussing the multitudinous methods for how to measure the impact of FTAs: http://www.adb.org/sites/default/files/publication/28929/impact-assessment-fta.pdf

23 Blind and Ziltener, 'Free Trade Live', pp.54-56

24 Blind and Ziltener, 'Free Trade Live', p.55. Extending the test beyond 2010 seems unlikely at present due to difficulty obtaining customs data from the Japanese side.

25 Blind and Ziltener, 'Free Trade Live', p.62

26 Watanebe, 'Free Trade and Economic Partnership Agreement between Switzerland and Japan: Review and Further Development', seminar presentation, Zurich, 10 November 2010

27 Shotter, J., 'ABB and Hitachi form Japanese joint venture focused on energy', *Financial Times*, 16 December 2014: http://www.ft.com/cms/s/0/0eb207a2-850c-11e4-bb63-00144feabdc0.html#axzz3ZM6xYXnT

28 'Swiss chocolate maker opens factory in Japan', *The Asahi Shimbun*, 14 November 2013: http://ajw.asahi.com/article/business/AJ201311140082

29 Corbin, D., 'How two Sri Lankans are building a robotic cloud in Switzerland and Japan', TechInAsia, 27 February 2015: https://www.techinasia.com/rapyuta-robots-cloud-infrastructure/

30 Monetas: http://www.monetas.ch/htm/655/fr/Publications-FOSC-Midokura-Sarl.htm?subj=2192474

31 'Takeda to acquire Nycomed', Takeda Media press release, 19 May 2011: http://www.tpi.takeda.com/media/news-releases/2011/takeda-to-acquire-nycomed/

32 Kijima, Y., 'Swiss firms prevail in Japan cosmetics market', Switzerland Global Enterprise, 26 February 2015: http://www.s-ge.com/en/blog/swiss-firms-prevail-japan-cosmetics-market

33 Iuchi, C., 'Japanese architects making mark on Swiss design landscape', *Japan Times*, 21 January 2015: http://www.japantimes.co.jp/news/2015/01/21/national/japanese-architects-making-mark-swiss-design-landscape/

34 Kashimada, F., 'Why are Japanese buying Swiss firms', SwissInfo, 15 June 2012: http://www.swissinfo.ch/fre/pourquoi-les-japonais-ach%C3%A8tent-des-firmes-suisses/32787988

35 'Toshiba agrees $2.3bn purchase of Landis+Gyr', *Financial Times*, 11 May 2011: http://www.ft.com/cms/s/0/b5d5c274-81e3-11e0-a063-00144feabdc0.html#axzz3aC0R3cBQ;
'Landis+Gyr helps create "highly efficient" Polish energy networks', PR Newswire, 6 May 2015: http://www.prnewswire.com/news-releases/landisgyr-helps-create-highly-efficient-polish-energy-networks-300077815.html

Chapter 5

1 From 'World Atlas' population statistics: http://www.worldatlas.com/aatlas/populations/ctypopls.htm

2 Simoes, A.J.G., and Hidalgo, C.A, The Economic Complexity Observatory: An Analytical Tool for Understanding the Dynamics of Economic Development. Workshops at the Twenty-Fifth AAAI Conference on Artificial Intelligence (2011). The Observatory for Economic Complexity website, created at MIT, includes an image generator that breaks down a country's imports/exports by

exporter/destination, based on publicly available data: https://atlas.media.mit.edu/en/. Data for visualisations after 2001 comes from UNCOMTRADE. The images offer a far more detailed interactive breakdown if viewed on the web. The visualisations used here split products by Harmonised System code.

3   OEC comparisons by author. The product types are from the Harmonized System tariff delineation.

Chapter 6

1   Lindsell, 'The Norwegian Way', pp.11-12

2   The enhanced Norwegian relationship is Conservative MEP David Campbell-Bannerman's concept of EEA-Lite, which retains Single Market access but reduces EU regulations applying to most UK businesses, dramatically reduces budgetary contributions, and replaces 'Free Movement of Persons' with 'Free Movement of Workers', reducing migration rights. See Conway, D., *With Friends Like These…Why Britain should leave the EU… and how*, London, Civitas: 2014, pp.125-139: http://civitas.org.uk/europe/WFLT

3   Chiavacci and Ziltener, 'Japanese perspective on a free trade agreement/economic partnership agreement (FTA/EPA) with Switzerland', p.30

4   Sampson, A., 'Australia's free trade agreement with Japan sees win exports boom', *The Weekly Times*, 10 April 2015: http://www.weeklytimesnow.com.au/agribusiness/wine/australias-free-trade-agreement-with-japan-sees-wine-exports-boom/story-fnlik0ph-1227296673677

5   Harris, R. 'Japan tariff cuts on beef to pass on millions to Australian producers', *The Weekly Times*, 9 April 2015: http://www.weeklytimesnow.com.au/agribusiness/cattle/japan-tariff-cuts-on-beef-to-pass-on-millions-to-australian-producers/story-fnkeqfz1-1227295633958

6   'Free trade agreement between Japan, Australia goes into effect', *Japan Today*, 16 January 2015: http://www.japantoday.com/category/politics/view/free-trade-agreement-between-japan-australia-goes-into-effect

7   Nottage, L.R., 'Investor-State Arbitration: Not in the Australia-Japan Free Trade Agreement, and Not Ever for Australia?', University of Sydney - Faculty of Law; Australian Network for Japanese Law, 4 May 2015, *Journal of Japanese Law*, Vol. 19, No. 38, pp. 37-52, 2014, Sydney Law School Research Paper No. 15/45, accessed at: http://papers.ssrn.com/sol3/papers.cfm?abstract_id=2602130

Chapter 7

1   This is further explored in Lindsell, J., *Softening the Blow: Who gains from the EU and how they can survive Brexit*, London: Civitas, 2014

2   See UK Treaties Online for a comprehensive list

3   This is a building block within the wider TPP efforts. 'Japan-Australia Economic Partnership Agreement', Australian Department for Foreign Affairs and Trade': http://dfat.gov.au/trade/agreements/jaepa/Pages/japan-australia-economic-partnership-agreement.aspx;
    'Australia, Japan free trade deal begins', *Sky News Australia*, 15 January 2015: http://www.skynews.com.au/news/top-stories/2015/01/15/australia--japan-free-trade-deal-begins.html

4   'Trade Sustainability Impact Assessment of the Comprehensive Trade and Investment Agreement between the European Union and Japan', European Commission, Draft Inception Report, prepared by LSE Enterprise Ltd, January 2015, p.11

5   'Trade Sustainability Impact Assessment', European Commission, p.12

6   'Trade Sustainability Impact Assessment', European Commission, p.37

7   They could benefit the likes of large UK employers like Jaguar-Land Rover, AstraZeneca and BT.

8   'Trade Sustainability Impact Assessment', European Commission, p.39

9   Chiavacci and Ziltener, 'Japanese perspective on a free trade agreement/economic partnership agreement (FTA/EPA) with Switzerland', p.30

10 They are both 'BRICS', the term first used by Goldman Sachs' chief economist Jim O'Neill to indicate that Brazil, Russia, India and China were the key economies to watch in the twenty-first century.

11 Lindsell, 'Norwegian Way'

12 Bradford, A., 'The Brussels Effect', *Northwestern University Law Review*, 2012, 107.1: http://scholarlycommons.law.northwestern.edu/cgi/viewcontent.cgi?article=1081&context=nulr.
    The phenomenon is sometimes called the 'California Effect' because Californian legislation has the same hegemony at state level.

13 Damrod, C., 'Market power Europe', Journal of European Public Policy, 19:5, 2012, pp. 682-699

14 Armitage, J., 'TTIP trade agreement: Critics driven "by anti-American sentiment" says minister Lord Livingston', *The Independent*, 2 September 2014: http://www.independent.co.uk/news/business/news/ttip-trade-agreement-critics-driven-by-antiamerican-sentiment-says-minister-lord-livingston-9705331.html

15 Observatory of Economic Complexity, 2012 data, counting all European states except Russia as being substantially EU-law applying for goods

16 'Trade Sustainability Impact Assessment', European Commission, p.14

17 The US imposed trade sanctions on Iran after the 1979 Iranian Revolution, which were expanded in the 1990s. The UN and EU imposed additional sanctions in 2006 (SC Resolution 1696)

18 'Japan, Switzerland sign open skies accord', *Japan Times*, 5 February 2014: http://www.japantimes.co.jp/news/2014/02/05/business/economy-business/japan-switzerland-sign-open-skies-accord/#.VWRy-U9VhBc